Putin Again

Implications for
Russia and the West

Philip Hanson, James Nixey,
Lilia Shevtsova and Andrew Wood

A Chatham House Report

February 2012

www.chathamhouse.org

Chatham House has been the home of the Royal Institute of International Affairs for ninety years. Our mission is to be a world-leading source of independent analysis, informed debate and influential ideas on how to build a prosperous and secure world for all.

The Royal Institute of International Affairs
Chatham House
10 St James's Square
London SW1Y 4LE
T: +44 (0) 20 7957 5700
F: + 44 (0) 20 7957 5710
www.chathamhouse.org

Charity Registration No. 208223

ISBN 978 1 86203 258 3

A catalogue record for this title is available from the British Library.

Designed and typeset by Soapbox, www.soapbox.co.uk

Printed and bound in Great Britain by Latimer Trend and Co Ltd

The material selected for the printing of this report is Elemental Chlorine Free and has been sourced from well-managed forests. It has been manufactured by an ISO 14001 certified mill under EMAS.

Contents

About the Authors   v

Acknowledgments   v

Executive Summary   vi

Резюме   ix

1   Introduction   1

2   Russia Between the Elections   3
Andrew Wood

3   The New Russia's Uncertainty: Atrophy, Implosion or Change?   9
Lilia Shevtsova

4   The Russian Economy and its Prospects   20
Philip Hanson

5   Russia's Geopolitical Compass: Losing Direction   31
James Nixey

6   Conclusion   40

About the Authors

Philip Hanson is an Associate Fellow of the Russia and Eurasia Programme at Chatham House and an Emeritus Professor of Birmingham University, where he also served as Director of the Centre for Russian and East European Studies. He has worked mainly on the Soviet and Russian economies. He is the author of a number of books, including *Regional Economic Change in Russia* (co-edited with Michael Bradshaw) and *The Rise and Fall of the Soviet Economy*, and of many journal articles. He was awarded an OBE in 2011 for services to Soviet and Russian studies.

James Nixey is Programme Manager and Research Fellow of the Russia and Eurasia Programme at Chatham House. His principal expertise is the domestic and international politics of Russia and the post-Soviet South Caucasus and Central Asia. Previous publications have included analyses of the wider repercussions of the 2008 conflict in Georgia, the decline of Russian influence in the wider Caucasus and Central Asian region, the Russo-Iranian relationship,

and a chapter on the South Caucasus in *A Question of Leadership: America's Role in a Changed World* (Chatham House, 2010).

Lilia Shevtsova is a senior associate at the Carnegie Moscow Centre, where she chairs the Russian Domestic Politics and Political Institutions Program. She is also an Associate Fellow of the Russia and Eurasia Programme at Chatham House. She is the author of *Yeltsin's Russia: Myths and Reality*; *Putin's Russia*; *Russia: Lost in Translation*; *Lonely Power* and *Change or Decay: Russia's Dilemma and the West's Response* (with Andrew Wood).

Andrew Wood is an Associate Fellow of the Russia and Eurasia Programme at Chatham House and author of *Change or Decay: Russia's Dilemma and the West's Response* (with Lilia Shevtsova) and a 2011 paper for Chatham House on *Russia's Business Diplomacy*. He is a consultant to a number of companies with an interest in Russia. He was British ambassador to Russia from 1995 to 2000.

Acknowledgments

The authors would like to thank Lubica Pollakova, Alex Nice, Dagna Drzazdzewska and Liana Fix on the Russia and Eurasia Programme and Margaret May and Nick Bouchet in the Publications Department at Chatham House for their assistance, persistence and insistence.

They would also like to thank the anonymous peer reviewers for their comments on the first draft of this report.

Executive Summary

The central message of this report is a warning: Russia's stability is at increased risk now that the 2011–12 electoral cycle is coming to an end. The overriding objective of Vladimir Putin and his team is to preserve the narrow and personalized ruling system that they have built over the past twelve years. The instruments of government, not least the security forces, are corrupted and unreliable, but they have a clear interest in maintaining the system that sustains them.

The ability of the resulting state structures to cope with the new social and economic pressures outlined in the report is limited. Real change, necessarily involving accountability and devolution of power, would disrupt the system. But without real change, Russia cannot develop as effectively as it could, and the Putin system is vulnerable to shock.

Elections and the domestic scene

The way in which the Duma elections of 4 December 2011 were fixed, and the implication that Putin and his team are determined to stay in power indefinitely, angered many Russians, including the country's educated urban electorate. The gulf between the rulers and many of the ruled was further widened. Only some 35% of the electorate in fact voted for the United Russia party, and 39% now say that Russia is moving in the wrong direction. Returning to the Kremlin will cost Putin his claim to be a national leader above politics and further weaken his legitimacy.

Although Putin has said there will be some economic improvements, Russia's ruling group has not set out a coherent strategic vision of how it will deal with the economic and political problems facing the country over the next five or six years. Meanwhile, those demanding change will have no legitimate means of promoting it. A tainted Duma and the prospect of a damaged presidency have compounded the existing problem of atrophied or blocked institutions to channel demands for change.

In several senses, the elections of 2011/12 mark the beginning of the end of the Putin regime. A next wave of protest in the Soviet-era provincial industrial cities, fuelled by social and economic discontent, is inevitable. Russians are beginning to flex their muscles as citizens rather than to behave merely as subjects, but opposition to the present regime which would follow clear, binding and publicly understood rules of the game has yet to emerge. This failure by the opposition to move on from protest to lasting organization is matched by the failure of the current authorities to reform the system from the top. The risk is that if the resulting stand-off continues, the consequences will prove damaging or even dangerous to the Russian state and by extension to the wider post-Soviet space.

The economy

Russia's economy needs systemic reform. But it is unlikely to get more than minor corrective surgery because the relationship between political power and business is too deeply entrenched. The economy is not actually in decline, but its prospects look disappointing, owing to its relative inability to deal effectively with economic crises and the likelihood of a volatile oil price. Poor economic prospects in the West, far from helping Russia to catch up, only compound its problems. International lending to Russian banks and companies is not likely to rise.

The declining working-age population may be the most important reason for gloom: Russia will probably lose 11 million members of its 102.2 million strong workforce by 2030 and it attracts very few highly skilled workers from abroad to compensate. Modernization in its wider sense – a better business environment, the rule of law, and institutional reform – would help; but there are few signs of this coming from Moscow's predatory officials, and excessive public spending is hindering long-term policy.

Foreign policy

Russia's ability to punch above its weight internationally is diminishing. This is true to its west, south and east. America and Europe are disappointed that Russia has not become a more responsible international player in the years since the end of communism. The 'reset' with the United States has been exposed as hollow, and relations with Europe are generally poor (Germany being a notable exception).

A lack of mutual respect and trust also characterizes relations with Russia's eastern neighbours. China, in particular, values Africa and even Latin America more. And along the country's long southern rim, the Soviet Union's 15 other successor states are all, to varying degrees, slipping through Moscow's fingers, diversifying their foreign policies at best and rejecting Russia outright at worst. The Arctic north is a promising area for Russia to exercise international influence, though its reactions to the region's increasingly globalized geopolitics are still unknown. Russia's desire to be a meaningful actor on the international stage contrasts strongly with the way it is seen by others as a self-interested spoiler.

The future

No one vision of the future is infallible. But the authors of this report firmly believe that the possibility, even probability, of things going badly wrong for Russia during the next six years is real. If the governing elite cannot adjust to changing realities, and autonomous institutions are not there to channel the demands of independent actors, the consequences are likely to play out in uncontrolled and unplanned events across the country. This may well have unpleasant repercussions for Europe and the wider international community.

European and US leaders should therefore regularly revisit their understanding of Russia's trajectory rather than assume that it is sufficient to establish a good personal relationship with the Russian leader of the day. And their relationship with Russia should be guided by the following principles:

- To accept the claim of some Russians that their country has its own unique set of values is a poor excuse for according to Russia the right to act as it pleases. Western leaders can best help Russia as a whole, though not necessarily please its present leaders, by focusing on their own strategic objective of integrating Russia into a liberal world system and doing, as far as they can, what is in accord with generally accepted international principles.

- The West should not accept the premise that Moscow has special rights over its former Soviet neighbours, while they are living in limbo. To condone the argument that, as a Great Power, Russia enjoys a higher status than others in Europe is to let those others down, and works against the strategic objective of integrating Russia into a liberal international community of nations.

- Russia should be held as far as possible to its word. The country has signed on to a full range of conventions governing human rights and other international norms of behaviour, but its record in implementing them is mixed and the international community has been tardy in holding it to account. Russia's entry into the WTO will be a test in this regard.

- Russia's economic and cultural links with other European countries are particularly strong, but have not been transformed into a coherent political relationship. It has been easy for Moscow to pursue its aims by dealing with individual countries, rather than multilateral European organizations – NATO somewhat apart. Individual EU countries have proved more concerned to placate Moscow than, for instance, to address human rights issues. While it is unlikely that this situation will change in the near future, closer consultation within the EU on how individual member states understand what is happening in Russia, and how the West should react, might gradually improve European cohesion.

- The EU should persist, despite all the attendant difficulties, in applying to Russia the principles of its Third Energy Package. Consistent application of those principles might help to nudge Russian policy-makers away from their pursuit of 'energy power' – a strategy that perpetuates Russia's addiction to resource rents.

- The United States will find Russia more difficult to deal with on Putin's return. Washington will need to take Moscow's skewed view of the world into account, but beware in doing so of appearing to accept it. There would be advantage in removing irritants such as the Jackson-Vanik amendment which go to buttress Russian official claims of rivalry, even hostility, and in working with Moscow as far as possible in, for instance, implementing Russia's effective entry into the World Trade Organization. But Russia will not be swayed by US gestures designed to pay in advance for hoped-for future cooperation, and Washington would be wise to avoid language that treats Russia as a 'Great Power' and somehow in a separate category along with the United States.

- Western countries can best advance their strategic interests by concentrating on particular opportunities. Small steps, as others have argued, can have a cumulative effect where grand gestures remain empty. Trade and investment ought to have a benign long-term effect, provided always that Western firms maintain a properly ethical approach. In the UK the stock exchange listing authorities should ensure that Russian firms admitted to an LSE listing fully comply with the standard requirements of transparency and an adequate free float of shares. In general, Russian firms or private interests dealing with Western institutions should be expected to do so according to clear conditions conforming to Western standards.

Резюме

Предложенный читателю доклад является предупреждением о возможных сценариях развития России и их последствиях. По мере завершения в России избирательного цикла 2011–2012 гг усиливается угроза нестабильности. Ключевой задачей Владимира Путина и его команды является сохранение системы персоналистской власти, которую они создавали в последние двенадцать лет. Инструменты персоналистской власти, в первую очередь силовики, коррумпированы и ненадежны. Но они все еще заинтересованы в сохранении системы, которая отражает их интересы.

Способность государственных структур справиться с новыми социально-экономическими вызовами, которые упомянуты в данном докладе, вызывает все больше сомнений. Реальные перемены, означающие прозрачность властных отношений и децентрализацию власти, могут только вызвать их дисфункциональность. Но без реальных перемен Россия не сможет эффективно развиваться, а система персоналистской власти оказывается уязвимой для любого вида шоков.

Выборы и внутренняя политика

Фальсификация результатов выборов в Думу 4 декабря 2011 г., только подтвердившая, что Путин и его команда намерены оставаться у власти бесконечно, возмутила многих россиян и в первую очередь образованный городской электорат. Произошло углубление пропасти между правящей группой и значительной частью общества. Прокремлевскую партию «Единая Россия» поддержали только около 35% избирателей, а 39% опрошенных россиян заявляют, что Россия движется «в неправильном направлении». Возвращение Путина в Кремль в таком контексте лишает его права претендовать на роль общенационального лидера, «стоящего над обществом», и еще больше ослабляет его легитимность.

Несмотря на постоянные обещания Владимира Путина улучшить социально-экономическую ситуацию, правящая группировка так и не предложила России четкое стратегическое видение и программу на ближайшие пять-шесть лет. Тем временем те, кто требует перемен, не имеют легальных средств их осуществить либо участвовать в них. Потерявшая легитимность в результате нечестных выборов Дума и перспектива дискредитации президентства только усугубили проблему атрофированных либо разрушенных институтов, которые должны быть средством перемен ...

Выборы 2011/12 стали началом конца путинского режима. Следующая волна протеста в промышленных центрах советской эпохи, имеющая социально-экономический характер, неизбежна. Россияне начинают ощущать себя в роли граждан, а не в роли подданных. Правда, еще предстоит консолидироваться антисистемной оппозиции, которая предложит обществу новые и понятные правила игры. Пока же мы видим неспособность оппозиции перейти от демонстрации протеста к эффективной организации и одновременно неспособность действующей власти реформировать систему сверху. Последствия этой ситуации порождают риски для будущего российской государственности и даже для всего постсоветского пространства.

Экономика

Экономика России нуждается в системных реформах. Но маловероятно, что власти пойдут на нечто большее, чем незначительная коррекция. Дело в том, что слияние власти и собственности настолько глубоко, что экономическая реформа невозможна без политических перемен. Пока нельзя говорить об упадке экономики. Но ее перспективы не вдохновляют прежде всего потому, что она неспособна эффективно противостоять экономическим кризисам и зависит от неустойчивой цены на нефть. Неблагоприятные экономические перспективы на Западе не только не дают России возможность догнать либеральные демократии, но и усугубляют ее собственные проблемы. Более того, вряд ли возможно достаточное международное кредитование российских банков и компаний.

Снижение численности населения трудоспособного возраста может оказаться одной из самых серьезных причин для уныния: Россия к 2030 году, скорее всего, потеряет 11 миллионов из своих 102, 2 миллионов работников. Страна привлекает ограниченное число высококвалифицированных кадров из-за рубежа и не может компенсировать нехватку квалифицированных кадров. Здесь помогла бы модернизация в широком смысле – улучшение бизнес-среды, верховенство закона и институциональные реформы. Но почти нет признаков того, что российский чиновничий класс, известный своими хищническими инстинктами, готов к такой модернизации. А чрезмерные государственные расходы не дают возможности формировать долгосрочную политику, основанную на национальных интересах.

Внешняя политика

Вызывает сомнения способность России выступать в серьезной весовой категории на международном уровне. Ослабление международной активности России ощущается на западном, южном и восточном направлениях. Америка и Европа разочарованы тем, что после падения коммунизма Россия так и не стала более ответственным международным игроком. «Перезагрузка» отношений с США оказалась лишенной конкретного содержания, а отношения с Европой оставляют желать лучшего (хотя отметим и заметное исключение – отношения России с Германией).

Отсутствие взаимного уважения и доверия характеризует отношения России с ее восточными

соседями. Так, Китай гораздо выше ценит свои отношения с Африкой и даже Латинской Америкой. На южных границах России новые независимые государства – преемники советских республик, пусть и в разной степени, но пытаются высвободиться из-под влияния Москвы, в лучшем случае выбирая многовекторную внешнюю политику, а в худшем случае и вовсе игнорируя Россию. Арктический Север – перспективное направление для осуществления международного влияния России, хотя ее реакция на усиливающуюся глобализацию этого региона остается весьма неопределенной. Желание России быть значимым игроком на международной арене резко контрастирует с тем, как на Россию смотрят другие международные акторы – нередко как страну-спойлера с эгоистичными интересами.

Будущее

Любое видение будущего не может претендовать на истину. Тем не менее, авторы доклада полагают, что существует реальная угроза того, что в ближайшие шесть лет Россия может оказаться перед лицом серьезных угроз. Если правящая элита не сможет приспособиться к меняющимся реалиям и в стране не будут созданы независимые институты, которые бы смогли артикулировать интересы общества, не исключено, что эта ситуация приведет к неконтролируемому ходу событий. Такой сценарий вполне может иметь негативные последствия для Европы и всего международного сообщества.

Европейские и американские лидеры должны постоянно уточнять свое понимание траектории России. Они должны преодолеть иллюзию, что для нормальных отношений с Россией достаточно установить хорошие личные отношения с российским лидером. Отношения Запада с Россией должны основываться на следующих принципах:

- Западное сообщество не может поддерживать утверждения, согласно которым Россия обладает собственным уникальным набором ценностей. Такие утверждения являются неубедительным оправданием для российской элиты действовать по своему усмотрению. Западные лидеры могут гораздо лучше помочь России, пусть и вопреки ожиданиям ее лидеров, сосредоточив внимание на задаче интеграции России в либеральную мировую систему в соответствии с общепринятыми международными принципами.

- Запад не должен поддерживать претензии Москва на особые права в отношении бывших советских республик, что заставляет их жить в подвешенном состоянии. Оправдывать аргумент, что, будучи «Великой Державой», Россия имеет более высокий статус, чем другие европейские государства, – означает согласиться с ущемленным статусом этих «других» государств. Такая позиция препятствует интеграции России в либеральное международное сообщество наций.

- Необходимо убедить Россию держать свое слово. Страна подписала весь набор международных конвенций, регулирующих права человека и другие международные нормы поведения. Но ее послужной список в их реализации является противоречивым и международное сообщество явно запаздывает со своими требованиями объяснений по этому поводу. Вступление России во Всемирную Торговую Организацию (ВТО) будет важным испытанием Москвы на способность соблюдать международные нормы.

- Весьма сильны и устойчивы экономические и культурные связи России с другими европейскими странами. Однако, они не были преобразованы в устойчивые политические отношения. Москва предпочитает преследовать свои цели, имея дело с отдельными странами, а не с многосторонними европейскими организациями – НАТО в некоторой степени занимает особое положение. В свою очередь оказалось, что отдельные страны ЕС больше волнует то, чтобы не раздражать Москву, чем, например, решение вопросов прав человека. Маловероятно, что эта ситуация изменится в ближайшем будущем. Но все же более тесные консультации в рамках ЕС относительно того, как отдельные государства-члены понимают, что происходит в России, и как Запад должен реагировать на российскую политику, могут облегчить процесс постепенного достижения европейского единства.

- ЕС, несмотря на все сопутствующие трудности, должен настаивать на применении к России принципов его Третьего энергетического пакета. Последовательное применение этих принципов может убедить российских политиков отказаться от их стремления сохранить за Россией роль «энергетической державы» – стратегии, которая закрепляет зависимость России от ресурсной ренты.

- Соединенные Штаты должны осознать, что после возвращения Путина в Кремль иметь дело с Россией будет труднее. Вашингтону придется принимать во внимание искаженную точку зрения официальной Москвы на мир, но при этом делать все, чтобы не создать впечатления, что американская администрация разделяет эту точку зрения. Полезно будет устранить раздражители в отношениях с Россией, такие, как поправка Джексона-Вэника, которые поддерживают российскую официальную версию о соперничестве, даже вражде в отношениях России и Америки. Необходимо работать с Москвой, насколько это возможно, над полноценным вступлением России во ВТО. Но Вашингтону стоит подумать над тем, чтобы отказаться от проведения в отношении России политики, которая может восприниматься, как оплата авансом за желанное дальнейшее сотрудничество. Вашингтону было бы разумно избегать формулировок, которые бы были восприняты, как согласие относиться к России как «великой державе» и которые бы давали Москве основания считать, что Россия входит в особую категорию государств вместе с Соединенными Штатами.

- Западные страны могут лучше всего продвигать свои стратегические интересы, концентрируя внимание на конкретных возможностях. Конкретные шаги, как было сказано, могут иметь кумулятивный эффект, в то время как грандиозные жесты могут оказаться пустой риторикой. Торговля и инвестиции могут привести к положительному долгосрочному эффекту, но при обязательном условии, что западные компании сохранят этический подход к своей деятельности в России. Британские ведомства, регулирующие допуск ценных бумаг на фондовую биржу, должны обеспечить полное соответствие российских фирм, допущенных к регистрации на Лондонской бирже ценных бумаг (LSE), стандартным требованиям по прозрачности и наличию достаточного количества акций таких фирм в свободном обращении. В целом, российские фирмы или частные инвесторы, ведущие дело с западными институтами, должны осознать, что они должны вести себя в соответствии с установленными западными стандартами.

1. Introduction

As Russia moves beyond its latest electoral cycle, one marked by controversy and popular protest between the parliamentary elections of December 2011 and the presidential election of March 2012, it enters a new era lumbered with familiar personalities in the Kremlin and the same system of personalized rule.

The principal objectives of this report are to analyse Russia's present political and economic condition; to describe the issues that the next government in Moscow will have to address and to assess its chances of doing so successfully; and to consider what the policies of the West should be.

Chapter 2, by Andrew Wood, assesses the current political situation in the light of the election cycle, and explains how it has been reached. In Chapter 3 Lilia Shevtsova analyses the state of Russian society and the implications of continuing with the current governance structures. In Chapter 4 Philip Hanson describes the economic scene, and details the problems that will confront the next Russian administration. Russia's probable foreign policy decisions and developments in the coming years are assessed by James Nixey in Chapter 5. The concluding chapter briefly sketches some possible outcomes of the Russian government's attempts to re-establish its authority.

This report makes it clear that Russia's leaders and society are confronted with significant and mounting challenges, and that how these are addressed could have serious and wide-ranging consequences. But the West too is faced with difficult questions about what it must do in relation to Russia. Tempting as it might be for it to duck these questions, it must not do so.

Some say that Western critics, and particularly those in the EU, are not well placed to carp. Continued prevarication in the United States, and indecision in the EU – not only but particularly in the eurozone – have eroded the weight, such as it has been, of Western opinion on what is happening in Russia. It is not just those sceptical about the Russian government who have lost out; many of those who praised the achievements of the Putin era now look discomfited too. But Western failures do not invalidate Western views of where Russia is headed. The trouble is that economic difficulties in Europe, and to a lesser extent in the United States, feed the Russian authorities' claim to manage difficulties better than others, and encourage them to pin the blame for adverse international conditions on the incompetence of the West.

For Russians and outsiders alike, the question remains: 'How long can the system of personalized rule atop a society that is governed more by understandings than institutions exist?' There is a clear sense in influential sectors of Russian society that the stability that Vladimir Putin claims to embody is at risk and that the remedies are known in principle but hard, even dangerous, to put into practice. The benign evolution that Putin talks of means limited economic adjustments without change in how the country is governed. It implies maintaining the status quo, but in fact will cause the continued deterioration in Russia's condition that has led to the recent demonstrations. The regime has drained of independence what ought to be separate state structures, such as the legislature, the judiciary and Russia's federal components, while giving their incumbents access to tempting opportunities for enrichment. This means that there are no institutional channels for expressing rival independent ideas or ambitions, which is to the short-term advantage of the regime – and Putin in particular. But it has also made for a rusting machinery of government, and deprived Russia's leaders of the means to cope with new challenges. The next Russian administration will be at particular risk when those who rejected Putin on the streets in December 2011 and February 2012, and seem intent on doing so again, are joined by people from his core constituency protesting at economic pain.

By deconstructing the daunting social, economic and foreign policy challenges facing Russia, this report shows that the implications for the country and for the West are stark: Russia's very fabric, as well as its place in the world, is at risk. The challenges are the same for whoever wins the March 2012 presidential election, of course. Another presidential term for Putin, with his track record and his inability to overcome – or even admit to – these challenges, actually makes the overall picture of decline and fall easier to forecast, if not in detail. The West will feel Russia's pain as it often has in history – not merely vicariously as a partially interested observer, but directly, as Russia lashes out while in denial of its own condition.

2. Russia Between the Elections

Andrew Wood

Introduction

Russia's governing system is in deep and perhaps accelerating crisis. The events triggered by the country's current election cycle, with the elections to the Duma held on 4 December 2011 and a presidential poll taking place on 4 March 2012, have brought this state of affairs more clearly into the open for Russians and outsiders alike. To see why and how it may develop, this chapter examines the present political situation and the prospects for the presidential elections.

Where we are now

The rule of a 'strong man' is inherently flawed: he cannot groom a 'strong' successor, and his exceptional strength may be shown by events to be an illusion. The presidency of Dmitry Medvedev has showed the primary weakness of the Putin regime.[1] Medvedev had no means of appearing stronger than his predecessor and master. His liberal-flavoured pronouncements appealed to many in the West and some in Russia, but carried no executive weight.

The logic of the Russian system therefore required that, since he was not ready to give up exercising power, Putin should return to overt control in 2012. Russia's regular constitutional governing instruments, though already ill developed, have become atrophied since Putin became president in 2000, leaving no other safe choice. Russia's personalized power system was thereby shown up as incapable of renewing itself. Yet the question of whether or not Putin would allow Medvedev a second presidential term nonetheless haunted Russian politics from 2008 on, and with particular force as 2011 wore on. That prevented strategic decisions about the longer term while encouraging speculation as to what the future might hold. The result was corrosive for the country.

While by 2011 few Russians believed that, if Medvedev did remain in office for another term, he would be a powerful president capable of implementing the changes he had spoken of in general terms, his presence in the Kremlin had nonetheless widened the accepted field for discussion and provided a counterpoint to the harder line associated with Putin. Making Medvedev advocate Putin as the next president at the congress of United Russia, the ruling party, on 24 September 2011 was needlessly cruel. It also looked hasty and ill-coordinated. Neither the public nor the party was consulted. The 2012 presidential election was made in advance to look more and more like a legalized but not necessarily legitimate putsch by an entrenched and self-interested ruling minority.

That impression was heightened by the leadership claim in September 2011 that switching back to a Putin presidency after a single Medvedev term had always been the plan, which – if true – made the Medvedev presidency a con. The original idea was presumably for the announcement of Putin's decision to run for the presidency again to be made after the December 2011 Duma elections had produced a solid majority for United Russia. Such a success would have helped to maintain the image of Putin as Russia's national leader. But the run-up to the Duma elections was notable for a series of ineffective improvisations intended to consolidate support for the regime. Putin's decision to create the All Russia Popular Front was, for instance, an obvious attempt to

---

[1]   I have for the sake of convenience on occasion referred to 'Putin' as shorthand for the regime as a whole, as well as when I mean the politician as an individual. I hope it is clear from the context which I have in mind. But a reminder that Putin is the dominant figure in a small group of ruling persons with common interests is worth emphasizing from the outset.

restore the fortunes of United Russia, which have been in marked decline. The initiative was badly orchestrated, however, and all it achieved was to let Putin distance himself to some degree from United Russia and hand the chalice of promoting the party's waning prospects to Medvedev.

The Duma elections on 4 December 2011 were a heavy blow to United Russia, and therefore to Putin. The official results on their own were bad enough, with the party slipping down to under half the vote, well below what the ruling group had expected and what Putin had counted on to launch a triumphant return to the Kremlin as a charismatic leader. United Russia can still expect to control the Duma, particularly given the customary acquiescence to Kremlin demands by the other three parties with seats. But to lose so much electoral support despite unprecedented administrative pressure and outright fraud was close to a disaster.[2]

Medvedev and Putin, in particular, proceeded to compound that disaster, by claiming the elections were honest, sanctioning the arrests of the first protestors against the results, and then slandering those who took to the streets on 10 December, not least by calling them agents of the United States. Putin's language after the 24 December demonstration was less offensive, but he again made it clear that there could be no rerun of the Duma elections – understandably enough from his point of view. The next protest meeting took place on 4 February. Far from showing that Putin's opponents are losing heart, or becoming fatally divided, as the ruling group has hoped, it attracted considerable numbers despite the intense cold, and probably more even than either of its predecessors. The counter-demonstration organized with the help of scarcely disguised official sponsorship was half-hearted by comparison. A further opposition demonstration is scheduled for 26 February. The focus has shifted definitively onto Putin personally and the role of an over-mighty president, not just the flawed Duma elections.

The demonstrations were sparked by electoral fraud, but were fuelled by wider grievances. The first is that much of the Russian public is bored with Putin and his unchanging entourage, and is irritated by being taken for granted. The people want some control over their lives. That feeds into the overwhelming public grievance over corruption. Putin and Medvedev, and others in the government hierarchy too, have repeatedly promised to tackle this evil. But corruption in its wider sense, meaning more than the practice of 'cash for favours', is not just endemic to the system, it *is* the system. Because the rulers are unaccountable, beyond the law and free to hand down decisions as they see fit, so are the ruled where they can be. Appointing governors from the centre, rather than letting them be elected locally, has not made them honest or effective. Instead it has largely shielded them from their local populations while making them dependent on the federal leadership. The centre, on the other hand, cannot know exactly what the regional governors do. Nor for that matter can the governors adequately control their local bureaucracies. The media have often been too cowed to expose wrongdoing, and the courts are too compromised to act against powerful political interests. The system of presidential representatives covering a number of regions has not worked.

Rule can hardly be anything but arbitrary in a polity where property rights are contingent on having the right political patron. The important lesson to be drawn from the Yukos affair,[3] for example, is not so much that Mikhail Khodorkovsky and Platon Lebedev should have heeded the Kremlin and stayed out of politics, but rather that they did not really own what they seemed to do because the oil company could be taken away by the Kremlin at its pleasure. Businessmen at all levels throughout Russia have suffered analogous fates. The lesson for those who have made spectacular fortunes under Putin and with his endorsement is that if you know the right person, you can prosper, but that no court will protect you if you fall out of favour with the regime. This too is corruption. So is the notorious practice of giving the children of the powerful

---

2   According to the official results, United Russia won 64.3% in the 2007 parliamentary elections, compared with 49.32% in 2011. See http://www.izbirkom.ru/region/izbirkom.

3   Mikhail Khodorkovsky, the former head of Yukos with an influence on Russian politics, was arrested in 2003 and convicted of embezzlement and money-laundering. The Russian tax police filed huge claims against Yukos and the company had to file for bankruptcy in 2006. It disappeared as a legal entity and its assets were sold off.

lucrative positions, regional or federal, for which they are obviously not qualified.

Corruption in both this general sense and in the practice of extortion has grown out of control since 2000. As the leaders of the opposition People's Freedom Party, Vladimir Ryzhkov, Vladimir Milov and Boris Nemtsov, point out in a 2011 pamphlet entitled 'Putin and Corruption', five senior officials were dismissed in 1997 because they had taken an advance of $90,000 on a book – a figure that looks laughable now.[4] Plenty of bureaucrats in today's Russia have watches worth more than that. Those who should impose the law quite often work directly with criminal groups. As Medvedev put it in his address to the National Assembly in November 2010, the forces of law and order have themselves become criminalized.[5]

The reputation of the ruling group has also been damaged by the way in which the economy has slowed since the high point of mid-2008. Putin was lucky in his first two terms as president because rising commodity prices and under-used capacity in Soviet-inherited assets worked effectively with prudent budgets and the enactment of the sorts of reforms that had been beyond Boris Yeltsin's reach in the 1990s to produce growth of around 7% a year. But the global economic crisis beginning in 2008 hit Russia hard and has made the future seem uncertain.

As the years have passed, the claim that Putin had brought Russia stability after the alleged chaos of the Yeltsin years also became less compelling, and the question of 'where next?' more insistent. Public opinion polls have recorded an increasing number of Russians who say that their country is heading in the wrong direction.

These worries were fed not just by disquiet over the people at the top of the political heap – and indeed until very recently Putin was seen much as the Tsars once were, as a ruler abused by his advisers and therefore not to be too much blamed. Events in 2011 revealed more than the high-handed attitude of the ruling elite towards the population at large and its lack of understanding of the changing currents of opinion in Russia. It also provided further confirmation of the steady deterioration in the efficacy of the 'vertical of power', as Putin has termed his top-down and personalized system of government. The transformation of the militia into a police force in 2011 made no difference to the way the public regarded it. The continued deterioration of the country's infrastructure, illustrated for the general public by a number of air crashes, the sinking of a large pleasure boat on the Volga in 2011 and the wave of wildfires in 2010, coupled with the inability of the authorities to cope with them, further fed distrust.

Over the last couple of years there have been numerous recommendations for action, some of them alarmist in tone, from a number of officially approved Moscow-based groups, in part as a follow-up to Medvedev's 'Russia, Forward!' internet article of September 2009, calling for early and extensive modernization lest Russia face eventual catastrophe.[6] The recommendations of all such reports have included better law protection and adjudication, and whether directly or by implication a more liberal political system, as essential if Russia is to diversify its economy and avert stagnation. So far nothing has been done to implement such proposals, and few believe that anything will be while the current regime remains in power.

Capital flight, the emigration of the talented, ethnic tensions, increasing corruption, the moral crisis of the bureaucracy, and the deterioration of Russia's position in relation to its peers are all signs of a country in trouble. But the public dismay at Putin's selection by United Russia on 24 September as the candidate for president they would support and the protests following the December Duma elections showed something new. Putin is still a powerful politician, but now he is only that. He is answerable, not above politics.

The presidential election

It was widely assumed until late 2011 that if Putin returned to the Kremlin, it would be for two full six-year terms. He himself made vainglorious comparisons with Franklin D. Roosevelt, who was elected to four terms as US president. That belief

4   People's Freedom Party, *Putin. Korruptsiya*, 23 March 2011. Available at putin-itogi.ru.

5   http://www.kremlin.ru/transcripts/9637.

6   Dmitri Medvedev, 'Rossiya, vperyod!' [Russia, Forward!], Kremlin.ru, 10 September 2009, available at http://news.kremlin.ru/news/5413.

is now past. For Putin, the presidential election in March 2012 is now about the next term only, with a question mark over whether or not it will even last six years. The Duma is tainted by the way it was elected, and Putin by the fact of his having framed and supported the system that produced it. The immediate question is whether or not Putin can hope to win outright on 4 March with 50% of the vote on returns that have not been too blatantly doctored. Assuming that he does pass muster on 4 March, or three weeks later in a second round, there will still be the question of how Russia's personalized, top-down system can provide for a formal succession to the leader (a question that, incidentally, also haunts the majority of other former Soviet states). Putin will, in short, be on probation. It remains to be seen whether, come 2018, he will be electable for the following six years or whether by then he and others in his team will have found a comfortable exit in the event that they decide their present system cannot somehow be sustained.

As president Putin will have a familiar sort of Duma to work with from May 2012, with a United Russia majority, the cooperative Liberal Democratic Party of Russia led by Vladimir Zhirinovsky, Just Russia under Sergey Mironov and Gennady Zyuganov's Communists, who apparently do not lust for power. Since the Duma under such a party configuration is likely to prefer a quiet life to challenging Putin, who will hold him accountable and in what way? The only answer is the 'Russian street', in the sense of both public opinion generally and those who have been out to demonstrate.

Putin's claim to be the anointed national leader above politics rested on his commanding lead in the public opinion polls, and much of the regard accorded to him in the West rested on that too. But his numbers have been dropping, while the proportion of those now saying that he is not to be trusted has risen to over 40% – including some of those who say that they will nevertheless still vote for him. It helps, of course, that the other candidates for the presidency are relatively weak, making the eventual choice one between Putin and the unknown. Just to make sure, the Electoral Commission has excluded Grigory Yavlinsky from the race, for two main reasons. First, while he is not seen to pose a direct threat to Putin, votes for him on

4 March could tip the balance away from Putin and thereby increase the risk of Putin being forced into a second round. Secondly, his liberally oriented Yabloko party's observers produced so much evidence of fraud during the Duma elections that they had to be prevented from doing so again in the presidential poll. Golos, the NGO blocked and blackened by the authorities in December for its efforts to coordinate reports of electoral violations, has been warned to quit its offices in February, well before its lease expires and in time to complicate any effort to check what happens in the presidential contest. But whatever the official result on 4 March, and even if it is not so blatantly distorted as last December's, the fact remains that Putin's hold over a vital part of the electorate, and the educated urban electorate in particular, has been shaken.

There will be those, perhaps particularly in the West, who find analyses such as Lilia Shevtsova's in Chapter 3 exaggerated in arguing the direness of Russia's internal social and political situation. But what she writes reflects both in the rigour of its analysis and the clarity of its emotional colouring the realities as they are seen by many in Russia. The divide between the rulers and vital elements of the ruled has unquestionably deepened, and the willingness of the ruled to protest has increased, the more so as they have seen that there are enough of them to make direct repression a riskier option for the regime. Putin and others are right to point to divisions among the protestors, to their lack of clearly identifiable leaders, and to the difficulties (especially for Putin) in meeting their demands. But this has not so far dented their force, not least their moral force.

Putin and his supporters have their own electorate, and while it may not be a majority, it is a substantial one. The scale of the reaction to the 4 December elections seems at first to have taken both Putin and Medvedev by surprise. They took refuge in stout denial, refusal to engage in considering the underlying issues and, particularly in Putin's case, vulgar abuse, to which he is prone when rattled. Medvedev has since, presumably with some sort of nod from Putin but without his explicit endorsement, made suggestions for opening future elections to greater competition and put a proposal to the new Duma for a centrally controlled form of gubernatorial elections. Putin has, however, cast doubt on this approach. Such ideas have in any case not been enough to pacify the opponents of the regime, partly because their detail is unconvincing and partly because of distrust as to what might happen after the presidential elections even if they were enacted. No one can be sure anyway that Medvedev will become prime minister in May 2012, or that he would carry much weight if he did. His star has faded rapidly, whether as a powerful political figure or as a liberal thinker.

Putin launched his presidential campaign in the middle of January. The electoral rhetoric of United Russia in 2011 and Putin now has been long on promises but short on concrete ideas for putting them into effect. In practical terms that has meant and still means an emphasis on the short term. Russia's rulers have also raised spending on favoured causes in advance of the elections. For instance, the government has been generous to pensioners and favoured clients for some time, but the budget for 2012 was notably so, including in its greatly increased funding for domestic security and defence, a particular cause for Medvedev. Defence is lucrative for everyone involved in that sector, with an authoritative estimate by the Russian military reporting that 20% of its funding never reaches its declared destination.[7]

While he has not changed his basic approach, however, Putin has begun to try to steal the opposition's rhetoric without conceding the political and economic liberation that will be needed to give it life. He has started to put out a series of articles on his plans for the next administration, and called for public discussion of them. The first was a general overview printed in *Izvestiya* on 16 January that elaborated on the short draft of his campaign purposes issued on 13 January.[8]

The main themes stressed by Putin's campaign to date have been the progress made since 2000 and building on it without rushing matters, his plans to encourage economic development and diversification, increasing social security, promoting education and free but disciplined societal cohesion, maintaining budgetary control (without emphasizing the point), the risks to the world economy, and lastly his determination to ensure that foreign powers respect Russia. This is all very well, but it is both familiar and bereft of practical detail, and cannot therefore be taken as foreshadowing a fresh start by a reinvigorated administration. Putin has so far said nothing to indicate that he sees a need for political or economic devolution, or the reconstruction of the federal system. The strain of anti-Western and particularly anti-American feeling has been a constant feature. Putin has also made reference to the wealthy Russians who put their money abroad, even into foreign football clubs, instead of investing in Russia. Getting at the privileged, or some of them at least and particularly those who made their fortunes during Yeltsin's time, remains an option for Putin.

Putin issued three more accounts of his purposes to cover particular sectors in *Nezavisimaya Gazeta* of 23 January,[9] *Vedomosti* on 30 January[10] and *Kommersant* on 6 February.[11] The first one addressed ethnic and national questions in such a way as to combine condemnation of extremism with conveying that he nevertheless understood popular (meaning Russian) sensitivities. The second acknowledged the need for improvements in the way the Russian economy operates but stressed that this should be achieved through existing state mechanisms, with no bankable acknowledgment of the need for structural or market reforms. The third dealt with issues of democracy in a familiar way, arguing that Russia would complete its own version in due time. Putin has also called for public discussion of his ideas, while making it clear that debating them with other candidates is not on the cards: according to his official spokesman, he is 'too busy'.[12] This may be wise. He has a tendency to rant when pressed for answers, as he did to Aleksei Venediktov of the liberal station Ekho Moskvi on 18 January when asked

7   See http://www.reuters.com/article/2011/05/24/us-russia-defence-idUSTRE74N1YX20110524.

8   Vladimir Putin, 'Rossiya sosredotachivayetsya – vyzovy, na kotorie my dolzny otvetit'' [Russia in Focus – The Challenges We Must Face], *Izvestia*, 16 January 2012. http://www.izvestia.ru/news/511884.

9   Vladimir Putin, 'Rossiya: Natsional'niy vopros' [Russia: The Ethnicity Issue], *Nezavisimaya Gazeta*, 23 January 2012. http://www.ng.ru/politics/2012-01-23/1_national.html.

10   Vladimir Putin, 'O nashikh ekonomicheskikh zadachakh' [About Our Economic Tasks], *Vedomosti*, 30 January 2012, http://www.vedomosti.ru/politics/news/1488145/o_nashih_ekonomicheskih_zadachah.

11   Vladimir Putin, 'Demokratiya i kachestvo gosudarstva' [Democracy and the quality of government], *Kommersant*, 6 February 2012, http://premier.gov.ru/events/news/18006/.

12   See http://www.bbc.co.uk/news/world-europe-16526026.

if he would be discussing his ideas with opposition leaders. He gave Venediktov a great deal of revealingly prejudiced allegations about Georgia, the West, American ABM plans, and took a good, even threatening, swipe at Ekho Moskvi while he was about it.[13]

The optimistic might read Putin's comments to the effect that, in general, steady progress is preferable to the dangerous adventurism that he says his opponents advocate, and his denial that stability means stagnation, as evidence of long-term purpose. But there has certainly been nothing so far to prepare Putin's voters for the fundamental and even wrenching changes that any genuine modernization would bring to their lives. That is understandable, given the short-term pain that so many of his supporters would have to undergo for the sake of longer-term benefit to Russia as a whole. But such a lack of warning would make substantive changes in the next presidential term all the harder to bring about – if indeed this is what Putin and his team have in mind. Putin's underlying theme remains 'it's me or chaos'.

13   See http://echo.msk.ru/blog/echomsk/850032-echo/ for a transcript of Putin's meeting with the media on 18 January.

3. The New Russia's Uncertainty: Atrophy, Implosion or Change?

Lilia Shevtsova

Introduction

The protests following the Russian parliamentary elections in December 2011, the largest since the collapse of the Soviet Union, shattered a status quo that had taken shape over the last decade and signalled that the country is entering turbulent waters. Russia finds itself caught in a trap: the 2011–12 parliamentary and presidential elections are intended to perpetuate a personalized power system that has become the source of decay. However, the top-down model of rule and its 'personifier' – Vladimir Putin – are already rejected by the most dynamic and educated urban sectors of the population.

It is hard to predict what consequences this will have: will it lead to the system's disintegration and even to the collapse of the state through growing rot and atrophy, or will the last gasp of personalized power end with a transformation that sets Russia on a new foundation? One thing is apparent: transformation will not happen in the shape of reform from above or within the system; if it does occur it will be the result of the deepening crisis and pressure from society.

The perpetuation of the Russian system

Over the years, Russia's ruling elite under Boris Yeltsin, Vladimir Putin and Dmitry Medvedev has put together what looks superficially like a very effective model for preserving the traditional Russian system resting upon three pillars – personalized power, its merger with property and an imperial outlook. This 'trinity' has been adapted to the new global and domestic reality, and to limited state resources. A number of mechanisms are used today to keep the personalized power system in place. Chief among them are:

- Imitation of Western institutions (parliament, elections, political pluralism) in order to give Russia's autocracy a civilized veneer;
- A circumstance-based 'pragmatism' concealing incompatible ideas and principles that has replaced coherent ideology and principles;
- Comparisons with the 'bad' Yeltsin period in order to present Putin as the leader who guarantees stability and growth;
- A combination of carrot-and-stick tactics such as co-opting members of various social groups, paternalistic policies to buy people's loyalty, and selective use of force or 'scare tactics' to prevent the consolidation of public opinion against the authorities;
- Comparatively broader space for personal freedoms (e.g. the continuation of free internet usage and the right to emigrate) to prevent people from demanding political freedoms;
- A foreign policy based on the principle of being simultaneously with, within and against the West, which makes it easier for the political elite to integrate personally into Western society while keeping Russian society closed off from the West by presenting it as an opponent and even an enemy.

Under Putin and Medvedev the Russian elite returned to its three habitual policies perpetuating the system that had been used by the Kremlin for centuries: militarism, attempts to modernize the economy using Western means and technology, and adherence to the 'non-accountability' principle.

With respect to militarism, the Kremlin realizes that Russia is not ready for a new confrontation with the West. However, the primacy of the state in Russia, which remains the spine of the system, demands the constant invocation

www.chathamhouse.org

of real or imagined threats, external and internal. Hence the need for a militaristic model to respond to these threats which determines the Russian state and nation's existence.

Today this model has exhausted its potential. But the Russian elite has failed to build a new mechanism to prop up the system, forcing Putin's ruling corporation to return to elements and symbols of a militaristic policy. The Kremlin is again attempting to consolidate society around the regime by projecting the image of Russia as a 'besieged fortress' and through the search for enemies at home and abroad. The 'besieged fortress' syndrome can be temporarily alleviated (as during Putin's anti-terrorist collaboration with George W. Bush in 2001–03 and during the 'reset' with Barack Obama, for example) or made to flare up if other methods for uniting the people around the Kremlin fail (as during the frosty relations with Washington in 2004–08).

Recent years have seen the use of many typical instruments from the old survival strategy book. These include the anti-NATO rhetoric[1] of the leadership and official propaganda, the attempt to transform the Collective Security Treaty Organization (CSTO) into a counterweight to NATO, rattling the nuclear sabre, militarization of the budget (spending on state defence, security and law enforcement will increase by 32.4% in 2012),[2] the constant emphasis on militaristic symbols in the Kremlin's public relations (frequent appearances by both Putin and Medvedev in commander-in-chief's uniform, or media opportunities for Putin in a fighter plane cockpit or Medvedev watching military exercises). The establishment of the All Russian People's Front and use of military vocabulary in the best Stalinist tradition before the 2011–12 elections are yet further signs of the authorities' attempts to revive the militarist outlook, which may look toothless but hardly help to build international relations based on trust.

As for modernization through accessing the West's money and technology, Russia has tried twice to use this model of economic and technological rejuvenation: under Peter the Great and Josef Stalin.[3] These attempts revived the economy for brief periods but ended with renewed stagnation. The attempts during the last 20 years to use the same strategy to modernize Russia without changing its political system did not bring even partial success. Spreading the use of new-generation technology requires a free society and free individuals. The pitiful attempt to establish a closed 'modernization zone' in Skolkovo confirms that the old model for re-energizing monopolized power no longer works. Skolkovo itself looks unlikely to have much chance of success now that everyone sees how its 'godfather', Medvedev, turned into a political ghost.

As far as 'non-accountability' is concerned, this requires that the leader is formally placed on a pedestal as the sole legitimate political player. He stands above the Russian political scene and is the only one who has all the means and instruments and levers of power. At the same time he shirks responsibility in order to survive. The leader would otherwise be answerable for every failure of the bureaucracy from top to bottom.

The announcement on 24 September 2011 of Putin's intention to return to the Kremlin seems on the outside to signify continuity of the status quo. But in reality this will lead to the same leader with the same view on power being confronted by the new domestic and global circumstances, and the old system will be faced with new risks and challenges with which it is unlikely to be able to cope. The old 'Putin consensus' – based on comparisons with a pathetic, inadequate Yeltsin and constant reminders of how difficult the 1990s were, fuelled by high oil prices, promising uninterrupted economic growth and unlimited resources for a patrimonial state – has started to crumble.[4]

---

1   'Putin slams NATO on Libya attacks', 26 April 2011, http://en.rian.ru/world/20110426/163721016.html.

2   Overall, as the Kremlin announced, total military expenditure in Russia up to 2020 will be $741 billion. Spending on national defence in 2012 will amount to 14.6% of the budget (in 2013, 17%; in 2014, 18.8%), and on national security and law enforcement it will amount in 2012 to 14.4% (in 2013, 14.4%; in 2014, 14.2%). Spending on the national economy in 2012 will be 14.2% (in 2013, 12.5; in 2014, 11.3%). Putin pledged a $688 billion increase in military spending until 2020. Education expenditure will amount in 2012 to 4.7% (in 2013, 4%; in 2014, 3.4%) and spending on heath care to 4.4% (in 2013, 3.7%; in 2014, 3.2%). 'Proekt Zakona o Federalnom Byudzete 2012–2014 ot 30.09.2011' [A draft law on the 2012–2014 federal budget, 30.09.2011], *Novaya Gazeta*, 11 November 2011.

3   Under Peter III, Catherine the Great, Alexander II and Piotr Stolypin, Russia tried to borrow Western principles of governance. However, these efforts only gave the Russian autocracy a new lease of life.

4   Weeks before the elections, Russians were increasingly voicing their displeasure with the party in power, as reflected in declining poll numbers for United Russia, Putin and Medvedev. In November 2011 only 31% of respondents said they would vote for Putin 'if the elections were held next Sunday', down from 70% in 2005. 'Vybory Presidenta' [The Presidential Elections], http://www.levada.ru/25-11-2011/vybory-prezidenta.

How continuity could rock the boat

Even before the December 2011 protests it was clear that the variables that have so far helped the Russian system stay afloat are now accelerating its decline. The mechanism that Arnold Toynbee defined as 'suicidal statecraft' has gone into action: the system, in attempting to deal with new challenges by using old methods, is undermining itself.

Russia's imitation of democratic institutions, especially the holding of elections, enables the ruling team to keep the regime in place and lay claims to a democratic image. But at the same time, blatant manipulation of democratic institutions that became the trademark of the Putin's regime, such as took place in the 2009 Moscow regional elections and the 2011 Duma elections, started to erode the legitimacy of authorities that have no other mechanisms (in particular inheritance-based or ideological) to justify their hold on power. The fact that more than 72% of Russians before the 2011 Duma elections said that they 'did not have an impact on the outcomes' and 'don't believe anyone', and that the results would be falsified, meant that people have no doubts about the real nature of Russian power.[5]

The commodities-based economy keeps the system propped up while also causing its rot. Russia completely fits the pattern of decline that has befallen other petro-states which had not democratized before their commodities boom began. Tamed and obedient institutions (with a rubber-stamp parliament, courts controlled by the executive power, and rigged elections) ensure an apparent calm, but the lack of channels through which people can express their various interests leaves them with no choice but to take to the streets. For now, the Kremlin's 'carrot and stick' tactic is still working, drawing various parts of society into the authorities' orbit, neutralizing and marginalizing those who reject the status quo. This process of putting society into an induced coma suppresses its energy.

In the absence of legally codified rules, corruption in Russia[6] became a form of cosy transaction between people, between society and authorities, and for some time guaranteed a mutually accepted way of life. But gradually corruption started to block any decision-making process; it disrupts the presidential pyramid of power. Even more important is the fact a growing part of society rejects the 'transactional pact' with bureaucracy, which instead of guaranteeing stability is triggering popular outrage.

Putin's eventual return to the Kremlin has been matched by efforts to reinforce myths to justify one-man rule. Particular energy has gone into arguing that the 'new' Putin or 'Putin 2.0' will be forced to carry out change, however unwillingly, and therefore must be supported. 'Putin still could become the reformer under pressure of tough reality!', the fans of personalized power would insist. At the same time the Kremlin ideologues, together with 'systemic liberals' loyal to the Kremlin (for instance Anatolii Chubais, German Gref, Alexei Kudrin or Arkadii Dvorkovich), or those who still sincerely believe in the Kremlin reformist potential, try hard to justify the need for gradual reform from above.[7]

Russia's reality makes these theories look dubious. If Putin is destined to become the transformer of Russian society, why did he not transform it earlier? Certainly, leaders can change their course under pressure but in Russia's case it is a change of system and not simply a change of course that is needed. Russia needs transformation, not reform that could make autocracy more effective. For real transformation to succeed, Putin's team would have to renounce its monopoly on power, which is the main source of the country's degradation, and open itself to competition. It would have to perform political hara-kiri. It is hard to imagine Putin announcing: 'I am leaving and I ask the parliament to reject all repressive laws we endorsed that limit political competition, and we are starting to prepare for new and free elections.'

---

5   'Vybory v Dumu' [The Duma Elections], http://www.levada.ru/25-11-2011/vybory-v-gosdumu.

6   According to Transparency International, Russia ranks 143rd out of 183 states, between Uganda and Nigeria, in the Corruption Perceptions Index 2011 (http://independent-news.ru/?p=18763). Independent sources claim that since 1992 Russia has lost $3.17 trillion owing to the corruption of state officials and business people, and during the last few years corruption has accounted for 27% of its GDP (http://www.korrup.ru/index.php?s=5&id=341).

7   See *Russia in the 21st Century: Vision for the Future,* Report of the Institute of Contemporary Development, http://www.insor-russia.ru/files/INSOR%20Russia%20in%20the%2021st%20century_ENG.pdf.

Instead, Putin's intention to return to the Kremlin shows that his team wants to keep hold of its monopoly. For the ruling team, leaving the Kremlin would mean not only losing control of assets but a threat to personal security. There is no doubt that the Russian authorities have followed the events of Arab Spring closely and drawn the conclusion that losing their hold on power risks their ending up like Hosni Mubarak or Muammar Gaddafi. Russia's leaders do not want to become another illustration in the story of how pathetically authoritarianism ends. But the more they keep hold of the Kremlin, the more they make the end inevitable and unpleasant.

As for the idea of authoritarian modernization from above in the economy, the authorities have been attempting to implement it over the last few years, but with what results? How can one carry out economic liberalization while strengthening the state's monopoly and control over the economy? How do you fight corruption if you turn the parliament into a circus and bury independent courts and the media?

One cannot but be amazed at the naivety or idealism of those who continue to believe in gradual reform, as if belief could help this happen. Supporters of the gradual path, for instance, assert that reform should begin in selected areas such as education, healthcare and agriculture, and only then spread further.[8] But how do you reform these sectors without de-monopolizing them and opening them to competition, and without the rule of law and independent courts? The authorities' continued monopoly on power makes any real reform impossible, even in just these limited sectors.

The authorities' tactical manoeuvres and the myths spread by the Kremlin propagandists can no longer stave off the crisis that has already begun. The system's adaptability has started to wear out. The system cannot guarantee Russians personal security, further economic wellbeing or a sense of dignity. It works only to satisfy entrenched interest groups at the expense of society. In fact, the status quo in Russia is only speeding up the degeneration of the system. Paradoxically, attempts to update this system by limiting personalized rule threaten to break it down altogether, as happened with the Soviet Union in 1991 when Gorbachev had liquidated the leading role of the Communist party.

The road to the inevitable: too little, too late?

The logic of decay has started its work in Russia and the unchanging leader and ruling team are doing their best to accelerate it. Many of those who at the beginning liked and even worshipped Putin have started to loathe him.[9] His leadership now reminds people of the Brezhnev era, which in their memory was the prelude to the collapse of the Soviet Union.

One should not forget, either, the fact that Putin's regime does not only rely on the security and law enforcement agencies, but is made up primarily of people who have come from the special services or are close to them.[10] They therefore have an ingrained repressive (or administrative) zeal and are less ready to use political instruments and consensual policy. For the first time in Russia's history, not only are the security agencies free of civilian control, but they have established their own regime. The Russian praetorians – special services operatives turned bureaucrats turned oligarchs – hardly have a modernization agenda on their minds. At first they went after total political control and juicy chunks of property; now they look for survival. The Russian *siloviki* have one purpose – pursuing their corporatist interests at any price and with the utmost cynicism and brutality.[11]

---

8   See J. Yasin, 'Scenarios of Russia's Development for the Longer Perspective', Liberal Mission Foundation, 2011, http://www.liberal.ru/upload/files/scenarii_yasin_light.pdf.

9   The change of attitude is reflected in the decline of Putin's percentage approval rating from the 70s to the 40s.

10   Among them are Sergei Ivanov, currently head of the Kremlin administration; Sergei Naryshkin, Chairman of the State Duma; Igor Sechin, Deputy Prime Minister, and Vladimir Yakunin, President of the Russian Railways.

11   For the first time the economic expansion of *siloviki* became the subject for the open debate in 2007 when Oleg Shvarzman, in an interview to *Kommersant* daily, said that he represented the organization founded in 2004 that specializes in the massive takeovers of enterprises and corporations and is supervised by the '*siloviki* bloc' headed by Igor Sechin. *Kommersant*, 30 November, 2007. Anatolii Chubais, commenting on this admission, confirmed that the process of 'stealing the assets under the cover of the power structures is going on' and 'this development is extremely dangerous'; http://altapress.ru/story/13559?story_print=1. With the authorities' growing control of the media channels, the discussion of 'this development' became subdued and the topic is now raised only by the opposition *Novaya Gazeta*.

The authorities' obsession with personal enrichment – especially among those coming from the special services – is another factor accelerating the regime's decline. This obsession makes the regime more repressive as it defends its rights to the assets it has gathered, but at the same time this 'commercialization' of the state's repressive machinery speeds up the system's degeneration and makes it insecure. As a result, the *siloviki* lose their ability to protect the system effectively.

Of course, one should not go too far in viewing the Russian regime as an exclusively Chekist phenomenon. It is an amalgam of the Russian 'Chicago boys' (the Russian liberal technocrats who favour economic reform under authoritarian leadership) and the *siloviki*: the former have been building the Russian economy and managing it, and the latter have been in charge of other functions of the state, including control of the financial flows. Representatives of other social and political groupings play supporting roles. They include the communists who have become the sparring partner of the Kremlin during the elections, giving it anti-communist legitimacy. However, it is the Chekists–systemic liberals axis that is crucial for the survival and economic efficiency of the Russian system, which is discrediting not only liberals in the government, but liberalism as an ideology.

The posture, views and nature of Putin have exerted a crucial impact on the substance and style of the regime. But one should not exaggerate the personal aspect of Russian personalized power. The 'personalizer', i.e. the leader who might occupy various positions, though usually that of president, controls the state resources. At the same time, he is hostage to the growing state bureaucracy, which is his main political base. The existence of a powerful bureaucratic class constrains the authoritarian leader who becomes strait-jacketed by myriad trade-offs and commitments. The leader, of course, could free himself and become an independent ruler by rejecting the bureaucracy and appealing to society. But Putin, apparently, cannot risk this and he continues to stay within the 'bureaucratic-authoritarian' type of political regime. This

does not mean that another putative candidate for the role of Russia's 'saviour' will not try to escape the bureaucratic embrace and offer a purely autocratic model of rule.

The criminalization of the state, which is reflected in the intertwining of crime, business, law enforcement and security agencies, and the authorities, is another sign of decay.[12] Why can the authorities not clean their stables even at tremendous cost to the regime's reputation? It is not that the authorities are implicated in each and every crime, and are trying to dispel suspicions against them, but any clear-out of personnel and any real struggle with crime would undermine the 'power vertical' edifice the Kremlin has built. It would violate the regime's fundamental principle: *in return for their loyalty, those who serve it are guaranteed impunity*. This mutual back-scratching among the authorities and the agencies at their service, and the fusion of power with the criminal world, cannot be eliminated without restructuring the 'presidential vertical' that is based on total rejection of accountability and moral commitments before the nation.

The jailing of oligarchs Mikhail Khodorkovsky and Platon Lebedev in 2003 demonstrated another of the system's fundamental principles: *wield a strong hand!* This explains why, having made the two men an example of his total grip on power, Putin cannot now release them, for this would be perceived as the end of the Putin era. Business has become hostage to the system and can exist only if it plays by the system's rules. But even when it plays by the rules it still cannot protect itself from the authorities and law enforcement agencies, which engage in mass extortion. The use of force against business has become a distinguishing feature of today's Russia, and this makes it impossible to build an effective economy.

How the Russian system is ruining itself

A number of circumstances continue to mitigate and blur the Russian situation, creating the impression that the system can keep going. The commodities economy

---

12   The most glaring cases were the rapes, slavery, coercion and murders perpetrated by the gang formed by the member of the pro-Kremlin party connected to local authorities and law enforcement organs in Kushchevsky town (Kransnodarski region) and the prosecutors' gang in the Moscow region controlling casinos. See http://www.novayagazeta.ru/society/555.html and http://www.gazeta.ru/social/2011/02/16/3527826.shtml.

continues to pump money into the state budget. The government proclaims decent-looking macroeconomic indicators. The Russian elites, though aware of the self-destructive course the country is on, reassure themselves with the hope that trouble is still a long way off. In any case, they all have guaranteed for themselves safe places far from Russia in the event of a cataclysm. Constant squabbles and in-fighting among opposition groups and figures, egged on by the Kremlin, discredit the opposition. The authorities have managed so far to channel social discontent into nationalist sentiments directed against migrants and people of non-Slavic ethnicity.[13]

The nostalgia for empire still present in parts of the population also mitigates social discontent as quite broad segments of society prefer for now to sit patiently and endure in return for preserving Russia's great-power status and 'areas of interests'.[14] Finally, Russian society's deep-reaching atomization, the destruction of old social and cultural ties, the demoralization and also the growing depression (reflected in alcoholism, a high male death rate, increasing suicide rate and murder rates, the growing number of abortions and degradation of the family as an institution) also hold these broader segments of society back from active protests.

However, the evidence is piling up that the Russian system has a limited lifespan. The question is whether the system will continue to rot or will implode. This dilemma may sound too pessimistic and gloomy (even uncomfortable) for Westerners accustomed to a more civilized narrative and experience. From the outside Russia appears calmer and more predictable, and some even believe that it is evolving in a positive direction. This optimism only highlights how different the inside and outside views are.

Structural deficiencies in the system became more apparent in 2011 and the people have started to realize this. The myth of the sustainability of Putin's Eldorado has been dispelled. In a survey in the autumn of 2011,

43% of respondents said the country 'is moving in the right direction', and 38% said it is 'taking the wrong direction'.[15] The public showed no particular enthusiasm at the news that Putin was seeking a new term in office: 31% of respondents approved the move (these people make up the Putin regime's core support base), 20% were not happy with the idea, and 41% said they had 'no particular feelings about it' (3% did not know).[16] Thus people have started to look at Putin with either indifference or disappointment.

Putin's personal popularity rating may still be high, but this 'Teflon president' phenomenon has its explanations: people in Russia realize that there is only one real institution in the country – the presidency – and part of the population is not ready to abandon it for fear of the chaos that might ensue (though even this institution has been devalued by Medvedev's presidency). However, growing criticism of Putin's government and the country's general policy course shows that people have no real illusions about the regime.

By the end of 2011, 82% of respondents thought that corruption in Russia had increased or stayed at its old level. Almost half of respondents said they had lost rather than gained over the last years, although 51% said that 'life is hard but bearable'.[17] This willingness to endure and look for ways to survive rather than turn to open protest has been until now one of the main reasons for the country's apparent calm. But patience, at least in the big cities, has started to wane. Before the December 2011 Duma elections 25% of respondents said they regarded mass protests as a possibility, and only 21% said they were willing to take part in them. These figures may look negligible, but they mean that millions of people were ready for active protest.

The Russian public has not only become increasingly weary of Putin himself; it has also started to reject the system's basic principles. Only 33% of respondents thought in 2011 that 'power should be concentrated in one pair of strong hands', while 59% took the view that 'society should be built on the foundation of democratic freedom'.[18] In

---

13 'Kremlin Struggling to Keep Lid on Pandora's Box of Nationalism', 20 December 2010, http://www.eurasianet.org/node/62608.

14 In January 2011 around 78% of respondents expressed their support for Russia's return to the status of 'great empire' (with 14% rejecting this idea), http://www.levada.ru/09-02-2011/osobyi-put-i-rossiiskaya-imperiya.

15 'Reitingi odobreniya i doveriya' [The Approval and Trust Ratings], http://www.levada.ru/30-09-2011/sentyabrskie-reitingi-odobreniya-i-doveriya.

16 'Vladimir Putin i ego tretii srok' [Vladimir Putin and His Third Term], http://www.levada.ru/07-10-2011/vladimir-putin-i-ego-tretii-srok.

17 'Krizis v Rossii' [Crisis in Russia], http://www.levada.ru/18-10-2011/krizis-v-rossii.

18 'O blagopoluchii naseleniya I demokratii' [On the Wellbeing of the Population and Democracy], http://www.levada.ru/press/2011081003.html.

another poll 24% of respondents said that 'the interests of the authorities and the society coincide' whereas 68% said that they 'do not coincide'.[19]

The Russian system cannot even secure the interests of its ruling class, which explains why its numerous representatives prefer to have their 'golden parachutes' outside Russia. Francis Fukuyama has identified two key forms of political decay. The first is the failure of ruling elites to change outmoded institutions and their inability 'to perceive that a failure has taken place'. In Russia the situation is more hopeless: the majority among the elite understands the suicidal path it is on but is unable or not ready to change it. The second form of decay is the process of 'repatrimonialization' by which the ruling elite tries to pass its position on to its children or friends.[20] 'The two types of political decay – institutional rigidity and repatrimonialization – oftentimes come together', concludes Fukuyama, 'as patrimonial officials with a large personal stake in the existing system seek to defend it against reform'.[21] This process is taking place in Russia: politics and business have turned into the family affair of influential clans raised to power during the Yeltsin and Putin years. Neo-patrimonialism helps to secure vested interests but also increases the dysfunctional nature of the system from the standpoint of society as whole.

What prospects for an alternative model?

Looking at Russia from the outside as 2011 gave way to 2012, there were no visible signs of a state about to go into collapse, as was the case in the late 1980s and early 1990s when wages went unpaid, production slumped all round, administration began to break down and crime surged. With the exception of a few large cities, the situation across the country was outwardly rather calm. However, as the

December protests and Putin's dwindling support proved, this calm has been deceptive.

The December awakening was a shock as much for the Kremlin as for the major part of a pundit community that had been feeling the growing frustration and anger but had not expected the outburst so soon in the most prosperous and conformist communities. Just before the unrest, some astute and respected Russian analysts argued that system was 'fundamentally solid and durable', that 'it will not collapse, and it will not radically evolve', and that 'no serious threat to the regime seems likely' because the system 'suits Russian citizens well enough'. Most such conclusions were based on the assumption that Russians found a way to solve their problems individually rather 'than to challenge national institutions collectively'.[22]

Another popular assumption was that the elite and the population agreed to play along, following the rules of a game based on opportunism, hoping to be incorporated in the system rather opposing it. It was supposed they silently agreed to give the regime unconditional loyalty in exchange for paternalistic guarantees. It appears that those who put forward such explanations failed to understand that numerous social groups are not ready to make what to the analysts seemed to be a rational choice.

Polling surveys too appeared to fail to detect the change. According to a November 2011 Levada Centre forecast, the Kremlin's United Russia party was expected to get 56% of the vote at the parliamentary elections.[23] While the official results gave United Russia 49.3%,[24] in reality it did not received more than 35% and the rest was the result of ballot-rigging.[25] This indicates that attitudes towards the regime could be more negative than people are ready to admit openly and that there is much more frustration in society than one would have thought earlier.

19   'O pravakh cheloveka …' [On Human Rights …], http://www.levada.ru/17-11-2011/o-pravakh-cheloveka-interesakh-vlasti-i-obshchestva-v-rossii.

20   Marina Litvinovich, 'The Power of Families. The Government. Part One' (2011), http://www.election2012.ru/reports/1/ and http://www.newsru.com/russia/22apr2011/meg_corr.html.

21   Francis Fukayama, *The Origins of Political Order: From Prehuman Times to the French Revolution* (London: Profile Books, 2011), pp. 452–54.

22   Vladislav Inozemtsev, 'Neo-Feudalism Explained', *The American Interest*, vol. VI, no. 4, March–April 2011, pp. 73–74.

23   'Vybory v …' [The Elections to…], http://www.levada.ru/25-11-2011/vybory-v-gosdumu.

24   See http://www.gazeta.ru/maps/elections2011/russia.shtml#0.

25   *Novaya Gazeta* has published numerous essays describing how the 'fraud machine' has been working. See http://www.novayagazeta.ru/topics/12.html.

15

The protest tide was the spontaneous movement of representatives of the middle class, the expert and media community, intellectuals and the younger generation, mainly in the big cities.[26] The protests have had a mostly moral and ethical dimension. After a long silence, the issues of respect for the dignity of individuals and fair rules were introduced into Russian politics, which is a great advance. The fad that part of the glamour class, representatives of the higher echelon of the political and business elite, attended the first rallies proved that, unexpectedly, even they want to be respected and aspire to have a sense of dignity. Beyond a newly emerging thirst for morality, there is a quite rational explanation for this sudden and supposedly irrational non-conformism: the understanding that the Putinist system is not sustainable and will go down. In this situation it is safer to be outside the system and even in the opposite camp, and to let everyone know that one was on the right side when the first wave started. This explains why so many representatives of the ruling elite – oligarchs, bureaucrats, former ministers and political leaders, or their wives or children – were at the rallies.

The first wave of protest, under the slogan 'For Fair Elections', has been a systemic protest. The newly emerged 'angry class' demanded honesty and fairness within the existing system. Soon the protests started to become radicalized, fast acquiring an anti-Putin flavour and becoming an anti-regime protest. However, these developments did not undermine the principle of personalized power and the constitutional framework that supports this type of rule. Moreover, the developments in recent months have demonstrated a longing on the part of various urban groups for new leaders (for instance, blogger Alexei Naval'niy has emerged as the new political star). This still fits the old personalized paradigm of politics in which a charismatic leader is the key mobilizing force that stands above society. The first wave of the 'Russian awakening' happened too early and has hardly had a chance to succeed – if success is viewed in terms not only of getting rid of Putin but of removing the system of personalized power as well in the short term.

Notwithstanding what may happen in the future, there is something new in the Russian political atmosphere – an understanding of the temporary, transitional nature of the current regime and even system, a feeling among broad layers of society that they have no future and are expendable. In fact, in the view of various social groups and even yesterday's apolitical people Putinism (as the leadership and the type of regime) is dead.

For the regime there is no middle road, as some believe. Whatever route Putin takes – liberalization or crackdown – he will lose. The reason is not only that the genie of freedom and the search for fairness is out of the bottle. Even more important is the fact that the people have seen a leader who could be aggressive but whose aggressiveness is a sign of growing impotence.[27] The understanding of the inevitability of change and readiness to help it come is the most optimistic and reassuring element in the new Russian reality.

There is also a growing understanding that the change will not come from within the system, that it will be result of political and social pressure on the part of society and not the outcome of any reformist activity by the ruling class. One could wonder, of course, what the impetus for such pressure will be. Could a new rigged election in March 2012 play this role? Or will it be triggered by the decline of oil prices and the piling economic problems? Most likely, the alternative will be born out of a new protest cycle spurred by a combination of political and economic factors.

Meanwhile, the Kremlin is thinking hard about its defensive strategy. During and immediately after the December crisis the authorities at first used violence against the protesters as they had usually done before. But soon the decision-makers realized that they had to change tactics and they rushed into offering a conciliatory package of half-baked changes for the legislature and promises to liberalize party registration. The sudden decision of the oligarch Mikhail Prokhorov to register as a presidential election candidate (and his registration in the role of virtual candidate when opposition representative Grigorii

---

26   According to Levada polls, during the rally on 24 December in Moscow around 44% of the participants in the rally were 'specialists' (experts), 12% were students, 8% were business owners, 8% were heads of businesses with more than 10 people, 9% were heads of businesses with fewer than 10 people, 8% were office staff and the rest were representatives of other social groups. See 'Opros na Sakharova …' [The Polls at Sakharov …], http://www.levada.ru/26-12-2011/opros-na -prospekte-sakharova-24-dekabrya.

27   Guillermo O'Donnell once called this type of leadership 'impotent omnipotence', in 'Delegative Democracy', *Journal of Democracy*, vol. 5, no. 1 (January 1994), p. 59.

Yavlinski was refused registration) and the appearance of Alexei Kudrin with an offer to act as a mediator between the 'street' and Putin showed how desperate the Kremlin was to dilute the protest. It was apparent that the ruling team had decided to stifle the angry crowd by such embraces and to split the opposition, targeting first the liberal-democratic groupings that had been the most vocal protestors. The authorities decided to use promises and an apparent readiness to negotiate to strengthen the voice of cautious opportunists among the opposition. Old tricks no longer work. Ironically, the Kremlin's allies have started to look for ways to cut the leash: the majority of the presidential candidates who until recently were obediently playing their roles in the Kremlin theatre suddenly accepted the demands of the protesters. This shows just how deep the cracks in the system are.

In case the tensions grow the Kremlin has a few other carrots available. It can fire the most disgraced officials; it can start some cleansing of the government corruption; it can even agree to hold new Duma elections.[28] But there is one bastion that the Kremlin will never surrender and that is the monopoly hold on power. The ruling team will not surrender Putin either – yet! In case of need, it will be ready to fight for its life. The skyrocketing expenditure on the military and special services suggests that the Kremlin has been oiling the mechanisms of repression.

The delegitimization of the regime continues in the meantime. At the beginning of 2012 Putin and his team still had the support of provincial Russia but that has been dwindling and this process cannot be stopped. In a situation where the economy is stagnating and financial reserves are depleting fast, Putin would inevitably lose the backing of those still loyal to him – lower-income groups and pensioners. The merger of the revolt of 'advanced' Russia and the protests of 'Soviet Russia' could create a political tsunami. The problem that will emerge soon will be how to bridge the different agendas of these 'two Russias'.

Polls taken at the end of December 2011 showed that around 44% of respondents supported the election protests (41% did not) and that 54% were convinced that the regime used the elections to 'preserve its power'.[29] The polls after protest rallies in Moscow showed the growth of the anti-regime moods in the capital – 45.5% of Muscovites supported the protest and 40.5% wanted new parliamentary elections,[30] while 29% of Muscovites said they were ready to take part in future protests.[31] About 63% of Russians said they expected 2012 would not be calm. Nearly 21% said they thought that Russia would see a *coup d'état* and 56% said that rallies and turmoil were a possibility.[32] With a sense of foreboding, Russians have been mentally preparing for rough times ahead.

Russia's development in the near term depends on two factors. The first is the extent of resources at the disposal of the regime – its support within society and the financial, administrative and repressive instruments that could be used to prolong its life.[33] So far Putin's regime still has the means to reproduce itself through the presidential elections in March 2012 and sustain itself for some time. But the Kremlin will have to use fraud to guarantee Putin's re-election and this will reduce the legitimacy of the regime even further.

---

28   The proposed changes that allegedly have to liberalize the political system ('the Medvedev package') in reality will be cosmetic or broaden the Kremlin's room for manoeuvre. The governors' elections, according to Putin, will have to proceed through the 'presidential filter' (apparently the president will pick the candidates for election). The new rules for party registration (instead of 45,000 members the party to be registered will need only 500) will result in a mushrooming of new parties, which will make it easier for the Kremlin to control them. In any case, the new rules will not change the situation because the next Duma elections will take place in 2016. The same could be said about the suggestion to cut the number of signatures needed for the presidential candidate to register from 2 million to 300,000 signatures – the next presidential elections will be held in 2018 and even with the lesser number of signatures the central Electoral Commission could disqualify a candidate if the Kremlin wished this.

29   Georgii Ilichev, 'The December Polls – 2011', *Novaya Gazeta*, 11 January 2012.

30   'Moskvichi o protestnykh' [Muscovites on the protest…], http://www.levada.ru/22-12-2011/moskvichi-o-protestnykh-mitingakh.

31   'Moskvichi ob oppoziysii' [Muscovites on Opposition…], http://www.levada.ru/19-12-2011/moskvichi-ob-oppozitsii-i-aktsiyakh-protesta-vystupleniyakh-v-podderzhku-edinoi-rossii.

32   'Chego ozhidayut rossiyane' [What do the Russians expect …], http://www.levada.ru/29-12-2011/chego-ozhidayut-rossiyane-v-nastupayushchem-godu.

33   However, the Kremlin hardly could rely on the loyalty of its repressive instruments. Alexei Filatov, Vice-President of the Alfa Anti-Terror Veterans' Association, admitted that according to the polls among the law enforcement organs prepared for the Security Council, about 90% of the rank-and-file officers are critical of the authorities. According to polls conducted by the trade union of the militia veterans among police officers before the Duma elections, a mere 3.8% were planning to vote for United Russia and the rest were going to vote for other parties (mainly for communists). Thus the mood within the 'power structures' is far from loyal with respect to the Kremlin. Alexei Filatov, 'Tichi Bunt Silovikov' [Quiet Revolt of the Siloviki], http://www.echo.msk.ru/blog/alfafilatov/850938-echo/, 21 January 2012.

Irrespective of the mechanism used for getting Putin back to the Kremlin, he will face serious economic problems that he cannot solve without solid popular support. The Kremlin might manage these problems if it still enjoyed a dozing society, an oil price bonanza and a Soviet industrial infrastructure that was still working (albeit with problems), but it does not have these safety nets any more. If Putin risks undertaking real economic reform, he will lose his traditional base of provincial Russia, pensioners and the bureaucracy. If he continues with a paternalistic policy, bribing loyalists and allowing his apparatus to rip apart the country, he will accelerate the economic downfall.

The second factor that will influence Russia's trajectory is the readiness of the Russian democratic opposition to consolidate on the basis of a clear strategy that will not only set feasible tactical priorities but will recognize the need for the constitutional change that liquidates the structural basis for autocracy, i.e. the super-presidency. The new Russia has to move from fighting to gain a monopoly on power to the struggle against the very principle of monopolized power. That will help Russian society abandon its centuries-long search for a leader-saviour and realize that it needs fixed rules, not fixers. Regrettably, at the moment the anti-regime mood in society is developing faster than the political opposition can unite, even as parts of society and some opposition forces are still looking around for a new charismatic leader to mobilize them.

Conclusion

We are observing the beginning of the end of the current Russian political regime headed by Putin. The final act could take some time: dismantling the Russian matrix will be a marathon, not a sprint. The regime will fight for survival by using the promise of liberalization as well as intimidation and repression. There are powerful entrenched interests that will support it. When Putin's personal preservation is no longer possible, one cannot discount either a consensual change of leaders among the ruling cabal, with Putin leaving the Kremlin voluntarily, or a palace coup. Besides, the end of the regime does not

mean the end of the system of personalized power – a change at the top could give the system some strength to continue for some time. The demise of the model of personalized power that has been suffocating Russia for centuries can be expected to be painful and to have both hostages and victims.

The first protests can be expected to subside at some point, just as the new ones that will happen in the spring could fizzle out too. Part of the 'angry class' that took to the streets of Moscow may return to their desks if their demands for a fair presidential election in March are partially met. The Kremlin could make the presidential vote in Moscow more or less fair and compensate for lost votes for Putin in provincial Russia where the population could still be forced to accept falsifications. In the end the most pragmatic part of the 'angry class' may agree to a new trade-off with the Kremlin: cosmetic changes in the political system, such as new elections for the Duma eventually, in exchange for renewed loyalty. However, the conformism of the pragmatists is likely to be tentative and short-lived this time. Today they still fear violence and the Kremlin's repression, and many of them may choose to wait and see. But there is no doubt about the pragmatists' rejection of the regime and the leader. They feel the Kremlin's weakness and when the new protest tide comes, they will not hesitate to join it.

Russia will have to go through a political frost and the regime's attempts to tighten the screws. There will be a lot of dramatic falls and ascendancies – some political clans will fade and others will emerge; coalitions will be forged and will split; disappointment with some political forces will lead people to choose 'love affairs' with others. The regime will attack and back off, make reshuffles, promise, threaten and cajole. In a word, the usual tale of agony that has happened so many times in Russia's history will repeat itself. But the feeling is that the agony of Putinism cannot last long – either the regime will take the decisive step and provoke society, or society will take the decisive step on its own.

The only way to transform Russia's system is not only to get rid of the current ruling team but to eliminate the old triad of personalized power, merger between power and business, and imperial ambitions. Powerful pressure from outside the system will be needed to set a transformation in motion. Moreover, the post-communist elite built a system that lacks constitutional and political means of resolving the conflicts and deadlocks. In this situation revolution could become the only means to displace the rent-seeking stakeholders and restructure the system in order to make it open to the interests of society.

The political and social actors who would be ready to exert this kind of organized pressure have not emerged yet. But the fact that Russian society has started to rise suggests that agents of change will appear sooner than many hoped. They could emerge from among mid-level innovation-linked business, the media community, experts' circles, intellectuals and younger people from the post-Soviet generation. Until recently the authorities prevented any new political actors from gaining strength by constantly clamping down on or discrediting any sign of opposition activity. However, such attempts on the part of the Kremlin now might only stimulate the creation of a new transformative class.

If Russia fails to build a real alternative to the current regime in the next decade, the system may go into open disintegration. This would greatly complicate attempts to set up new rules based on liberal-democratic principles. The collapse of the old system and public discontent could bring about a repeat of 1991 and see the monopolist tendency simply regenerate itself in a new guise. Russia's political class and society do not have much time to find peaceful ways out of the current dead-end before the system starts to unravel.

4. The Russian Economy and its Prospects

Philip Hanson

Introduction

The Russian economy was transformed in the 1990s. It now needs to be transformed again. That is the view of Russian liberal critics of the Putinist order. They speak of a need not merely for reform but for 'systemic reform'. This was never likely to come about in the near future. The new political line-up makes it more unlikely.

Outside observers might be forgiven for thinking that systemic reform, altering fundamental institutions and working arrangements in the economy, is something that Russia has already undergone once, with considerable pain, and that the country could be spared a repeat performance. Unfortunately, the institutional changes that have occurred in Russia since 1991 are akin to a bungled operation. Russia has a market, capitalist economy, but not a very good one. The hope must be that corrective surgery can be carried out more or less painlessly. This is not easy to envisage, however. Nor is there any certainty that it will be carried out at all, painlessly or otherwise.

At the heart of Russia's 'systemic' problem is the relationship between political power and business. In this, it is not alone. 'Turning money into power and power back into money are Washington's two main industries,' writes Jeffrey Sachs.[1] But America's 'corporatocracy' (Sachs' term) and Russia's corruption and lack of a rule of law are different pathologies.

I begin this chapter with a review of the strengths and weaknesses of the Russian economy. I move on to a discussion of both macro-economic policy and institutional reform and then consider the case for radical institutional change, the changes being proposed, the chances of success under a new Putin presidency and the implications of success or failure for the Western countries.

Strengths and weaknesses

The economic difficulties facing the Russian people are less acute than those that face the European Union and the United States today. It would be quite misleading to say that the Russian economy is in decline or is doomed to decline. Only in some worst-case scenarios (of which more below) are analysts projecting a fall in Russian economic activity at any point within the next few years.

In 2010–11 Russia's economy grew at about 4% a year. Unemployment at mid-2011 was 6.5%. The current account of the balance of payments showed a surplus of $101 billion; the 2011 federal budget surplus was at 0.8% of GDP and consumer prices rose by 6.1%, the lowest end-year figure since the fall of communism.[2] Public debt was about 11% of GDP.[3] Per capita GDP in purchasing power parity terms in 2010 was $15,612;[4] this puts Russia comfortably in the World Bank's category of 'upper-middle-income countries'.

The problem facing the Russian economy is that its recent performance and future prospects are disappointing. They are a disappointment to the country's

1   Jeffrey Sachs, *The Price of Civilization* (New York: Random House, 2011), p. 237.
2   Ol'ga Kuvshinova and Yevgeniya Pis'mennaya, 'Raskhody byudzheta okazalis' na 200 mlrd rub. nizhe zaplanirovannykh' [Budget expenditure 200 billion roubles lower than planned], *Vedomosti*, 11 January 2012; Margarita Lyutova, 'V Rossii zafiksirovan rekordniy rost potrebitel'skikh tsen' [Record growth of consumer prices registered in Russia], in ibid.
3   Rosstat and Central Bank of Russia statistics, www.gks.ru and http://cbr.ru/statistics/.
4   International Monetary Fund, World Economic Outlook database, September 2011, http://www.imf.org/external/pubs/ft/weo/2011/02/weodata/weorept.aspx?sy=2009&ey=2016&scsm=1&ssd=1&sort=country&ds=.&br=1&c=922&s=NGDPD%2CPPPPC&grp=0&a=&pr.x=19&pr.y=9.

policy elite, to much of the business community and, to judge from opinion surveys, to much of the population. The ancient Russian custom of not catching up with and overtaking more developed countries looks likely, yet again, to be preserved.

Between the Russian financial crisis of 1998 and the global financial crisis of 2008 Russia's GDP grew at about 7% per annum. In 2009 it fell by 7.8% year-on-year. That was the worst setback experienced by any G20 nation. It was worse than the slowdowns or modest declines experienced by other large emerging economies and other major oil exporters. True, it was not as large as some of the declines observed in several smaller ex-communist countries such as the Baltic states, and Russia's leaders could derive some comfort from that. However, economic performance since 2009 has not reverted to anything like the buoyant growth of the inter-crisis period, and no forecasts, including those of the Ministry of Economic Development (MinEkon), envisage it doing so. This is worrying for a country with labour productivity still only at about 44% of that of Germany.[5]

Figure 1 shows both the recent record and one of the more optimistic MinEkon projections (as of early 2011) for the next few years. It shows year-on-year percentage changes for both real GDP and the average annual Urals oil price, on separate axes. The GDP projections are for the official 'innovation' scenario, so they end with an optimistic uptick in 2020. Before that the growth rate drops below 4% in several years. The projections of the oil price are largely conjectural and exhibit a lack of imagination. They show it falling in 2012 and then edging up very gradually at around 2% a year. If history is any guide at all, the oil price will be a lot more volatile than that.

The prospect of economic growth at 4% a year would be a cause for jubilation in the developed West. For Russia, it should, arithmetically, mean continued 'catching up and overtaking'. The snags are that the catching-up would be in slow motion, Russia would be dawdling by comparison with other large emerging economies, and there are some worrying downside risks as well. Household real income growth has slowed, along with GDP, perhaps causing some damage to public satisfaction with Russia's progress.

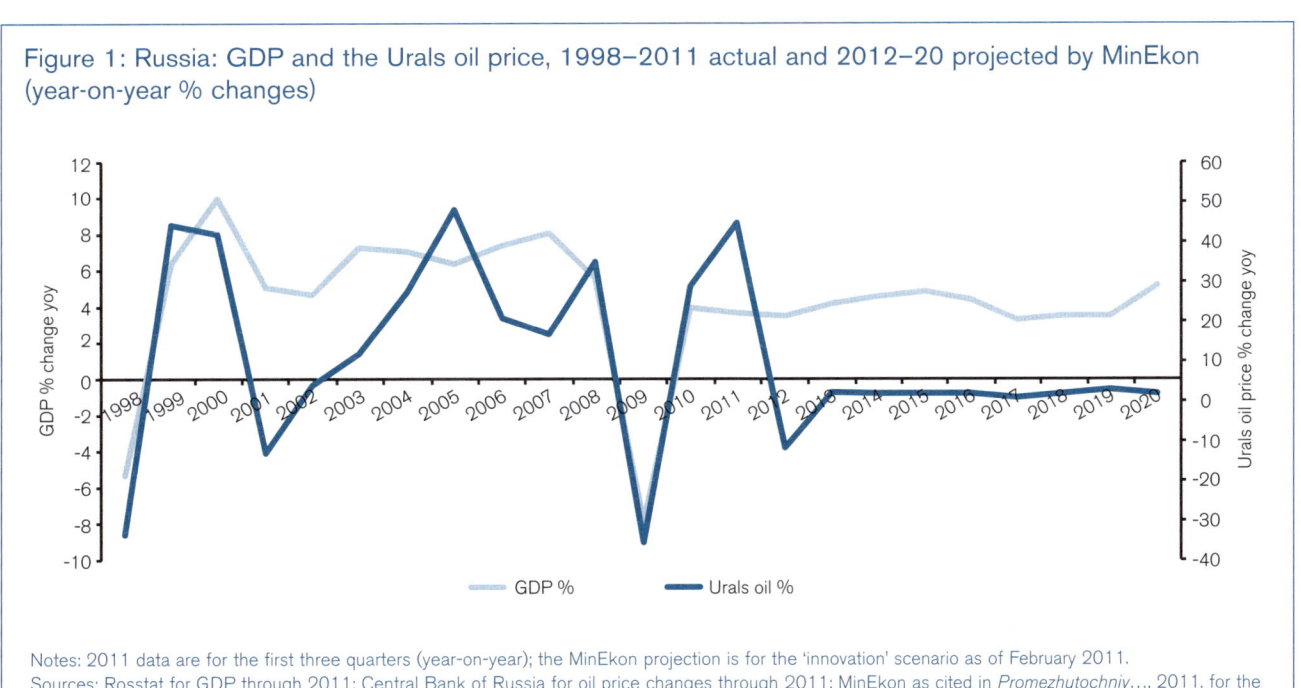

Figure 1: Russia: GDP and the Urals oil price, 1998–2011 actual and 2012–20 projected by MinEkon (year-on-year % changes)

Notes: 2011 data are for the first three quarters (year-on-year); the MinEkon projection is for the 'innovation' scenario as of February 2011.
Sources: Rosstat for GDP through 2011; Central Bank of Russia for oil price changes through 2011; MinEkon as cited in *Promezhutochniy…*, 2011, for the projections (see note 10 below for details).

5   Author's calculation for 2009 based on GDP in purchasing power parity (PPP) dollars from IMF World Economic Outlook database of October 2010, divided by employment data from the same source for Germany and, for Russia, from Rosstat: Germany $69,900; Russia $30,500.

Having already constructed baseline, optimistic and conservative projections through 2014, MinEkon in September 2011 produced a worst-case and an even-worse-case one. In the former, the eurozone stagnates, US growth slows further and the Russian economy grows at only 2.5% in 2012 and 1.5% in 2013. In the latter, the Urals oil price falls to an annual average of $60/barrel in 2012 and Russian GDP falls in the following year by between 0.5% and 1.4%.[6]

These scenarios illustrate something that troubles Russia's political elite: a double-dip recession or stagnation in the West is not an opportunity for the country to catch up but a reason for it to slow down. About half of Russian merchandise exports go to the EU. About two-thirds of all Russian merchandise exports are oil and gas, equivalent in 2010 to almost a fifth of GDP. Russia's economic prospects are tied very closely both to Europe and to the price of oil.[7]

Why has the Russian economy slowed down?

One possible reason for the slowdown is that Russia has got caught in the middle-income trap. Data for the period since 1957 show that initial fast growth in a number of countries slowed down by at least 2 percentage points a year when their per capita GDP reached somewhere in the region of $17,000 in 2005 international prices.[8] Characteristically, these slowdowns were associated with slowing growth of total factor productivity (output per unit of labour and capital combined). One plausible interpretation of this evidence is that these middle-income countries had reached a point at which easy gains from the flow of labour and capital out of low-productivity sectors into higher-productivity sectors, and also from technology transfer, had begun to be exhausted.

It is possible that this diagnosis also applies to Russia now. But there are some likely influences that do not fit the middle-income-trap diagnosis. They seem to be specific to Russia and to the present international economic conjuncture.

During the inter-crisis boom, Russia's working-age population was growing, the oil price was, for much of the time, rising, and in 2003–08 international credit to Russian banks (facilitating their domestic lending) and to Russian non-bank corporations was growing rapidly. These benign influences have since weakened or gone into reverse.

Demographic influences are perhaps the most important. In the inter-crisis boom, despite the fact that the total population was falling, working-age population and actual employment were growing, partly because of the age structure of the Russian-born population and partly because of immigration. Now Rosstat estimates that the population aged between 15 and 65[9] is likely to fall from 102.2 million in 2010 to 91.1 million in 2030, despite a projected net in-migration of 4.5 million.[10]

The sharp fall in young entrants to the labour force has three damaging effects on economic growth. It reduces the quantity of labour inputs. It reduces productivity-enhancing occupational shifts, since new entrants tend to be taken on in the more rapidly developing branches of the economy. And it reduces the rate of growth of human capital, since this is the age group that most rapidly acquires new skills.

On top of that, two growth stimuli of the boom period are likely to be much weaker during the next few years: international lending to Russian banks and companies is not expected to resume its rapid rise; nor is the oil price, short-term volatility apart.

6   Ol'ga Kuvshinova, 'Minekonomrazvitiya napisalo stsenariy novoi volny krizisa' [The Ministry for Economic Development has prepared a scenario for a new wave of economic crisis], *Vedomosti*, 9 September 2011.

7   Russia is nonetheless not as vulnerable as most of central and southeastern Europe to events in the eurozone. See the EBRD assessment of vulnerability in Table 2 (p. 7) in 'Economic Prospects in EBRD Countries of Operation', http://www.ebrd.com/downloads/news/REP_October_2011_181011_Final.pdf.

8   Barry Eichengreen, Donghyun Park and Kwanho Shin, 'When Fast Growing Economies Slow Down. International Evidence and Implications for China', NBER Working Paper no. 16919, March 2011.

9   The official retirement age is 55 for women and 60 for men, but many pensioners work.

10   As cited in the Interim Report of the experts engaged in revising the national 2020 strategy, *Promezhutochniy doklad o rezul'tatakh ekspertnoi raboty po aktual'nym problemam sotsial'no-ekonomicheskoi strategii Rossii na period do 2020 goda* [Interim report on the results of expert analysis of current issues in Russia's 2020 socio-economic strategy], downloaded from the *Kommersant* website on 19 August 2011, http://kommersant.ru/content/pics/doc/doc1753934.pdf at p. 163; henceforth referred to as *Promezhutochniy … 2011*.

The slowdown, therefore, does not necessarily mean that the business environment in Russia has got worse. It may or may not have. The recent and prospective slowdown in economic growth can probably be accounted for by the influences just described, without recourse to the notion of a worsening business climate.[11]

What could improve the growth rate, given these negative influences? Higher rates of immigration would help, but Russia does not attract highly qualified workers in more than tiny numbers, and immigration from the Transcaucasus and Central Asia is politically sensitive. A higher rate of growth of the capital stock would also help, but the share of fixed investment in GDP remains modest for an emerging economy: 20.5% in 2010. A faster rate of introduction and diffusion of new products and processes is another obvious candidate. It is associated in the minds of many Russian officials and politicians with diversification of the economy, with Russia becoming a 'knowledge' economy and in general a place to be proud of. Hence the political attention to the idea of modernization.

This is where the poor quality of the business environment comes in. It may not be the cause of the slowdown but it needs to be improved if the economy is to regain a more encouraging momentum. Without fundamental reform of Russia's economic institutions it is hard to see where faster growth of investment or of technological progress is going to come from.

Budgetary problems

Russian policy-makers face a more immediate and more tractable problem than the long-term one of a poor business environment: excessive public spending. If the federal and sub-national budgets are taken together, total spending planned for 2012 would be 39.1% of GDP.[12] Public debate focuses on the federal budget only, which is reasonable since sub-national governments can run only very small deficits. But it is worth bearing in mind that total public spending is rather high for a middle-income country.

The Duma has approved the federal budget plan for 2012 and the outline plan for 2012–14, and critics warn that spending is set too high over the next few years. The planned spending still depends heavily on the oil price. The annual average Urals oil prices assumed in the budget outline plan, of the order of $100, are plausible enough, but leave a large downside risk. At a $60 oil price in 2012, the federal budget deficit would be 5.5% of GDP, according to estimates by former Minister of Finance Aleksei Kudrin.[13] A deficit of that order may be viable for a time in some nations, but would be very damaging in Russia, where confidence in the economy is already weak. The Ministry of Economic Development estimates that this scenario in 2012 would be followed by a fall in GDP of 0.5–1.4% in 2013.

Kudrin's resignation in September 2011 has dramatized the struggle between fiscal conservatives and big spenders. He has argued that the state should give priority to rebuilding its Reserve Fund instead of doing what it is currently doing: boosting public-sector pay and pensions, re-equipping the military and spending on top-down industrial 'modernization'. The objectives of policy should, in Kudrin's view, be to:

- design a federal budget that will balance at an oil price of $90 a barrel in 2015;
- restrict spending if the oil price falls (by capping the 'non-oil-and-gas deficit' planned for the budget);
- review (and, by implication, cut) planned defence spending;
- peg pensions to the rate of inflation, rather than increasing them in real terms; and
- lower, year by year, the ratio of budgetary spending to GDP.

This is a serious matter. A Putin-led regime might be capable of dealing with it once the 2012 presidential elections are over, but recent political developments cast some doubt on its capacity to do so. The record on policy is

---

11 For more detail on this growth accounting argument see Philip Hanson, 'Russia to 2020', Finmeccanica Occasional Paper, November 2009; and Masaaki Kuboniwa, 'Russian Growth Path in Light of Production Function Estimation Using Quarterly Data', in Iika Korhonen and Laura Solanko (eds), *From Soviet Plans to Russian Reality* (Helsinki: WSOY, 2010) pp. 39–53.

12 World Bank in Russia, 'Russian Economic Report: Growing Risks in Russia', 14 September 2011.

13 Aleksei Kudrin, 'Bortom k volne' [Riding the wave], *Kommersant*, 15 October 2011.

encouraging. Putin tended in the past to support Kudrin's calls for fiscal prudence (although he overrode them in the 2007–08 electoral cycle, with damaging results for inflation). He has not usually been on the side of the big spenders. He may be capable of cutting, for example, the wildly over-ambitious military spending plans, even if Kudrin were not to return to the government.[14] Putin's loss of credibility in the face of the large protests that followed the December 2011 Duma elections, however, lowers his ability to reimpose fiscal discipline. He and his close associates are now more likely than before to find it necessary to appease the military, along with the other constituencies for big public spending. The question of institutional reform, therefore, is even less likely to find a satisfactory answer.

Table 1: Russia – EoDB rankings 2012 (n = 183)	
Starting a business	111
Dealing with construction permits	178
Getting electricity	183
Registering property	45
Getting credit	98
Protecting investors	111
Paying taxes	105
Trading across borders	160
Enforcing contracts	13
Resolving insolvency	60
Overall	**120**

Source: World Bank, Ease of Doing Business (http://www.doingbusiness.org).

The rule of law and all that

What is wrong with Russia's economic institutions? The answer is familiar. It has become something of a cliché to say that the rule of law and therefore the protection of property rights are weak in Russia. It is also true. Russia fares badly in the World Bank's governance indicator for Rule of Law.[15]

The World Bank's 'ease of doing business' (EoDB) index provides background information on the Russian state's excessive and corrupt intervention in the economy. This is based on survey data on the time and number of official procedures needed to negotiate legal and regulatory requirements, and the cost entailed, in a range of basic business activities. Table 1 summarizes Russia's position out of 183 nations in the EoDB 2012 rankings, based on 2011 information. Russia also comes out poorly in other such scoring systems – the OECD's product market regulation index, the World Bank/EBRD Business Environment and Enterprise Performance Survey, the World Economic Forum's Global Competitiveness Report and several more – as far as economic arrangements that depend on legislation and the quality of public administration are concerned.[16]

The argument that such survey findings merely show Russia to be 'normal' for its development level does not stand up. Russia is, in World Bank categories, an upper-middle-income country. Of the 49 upper-middle-income countries included in the 2012 EoDB rankings, it comes 40th.

Russian arrangements allow the illicit extraction of kickbacks and theft of assets by predatory officials and by businesspeople closely connected to them. In addition, informal links between particular businesspeople and officials, at the national, regional and local levels, are deployed by incumbent firms to keep out market entrants and to undermine established rivals. Regulation provides the instruments. State officials use tax demands, environmental and other regulation, and certification and licensing either to extract rents for themselves or to favour cronies.

This rent-seeking behaviour takes a variety of forms. The Russian word *reiderstvo*, for example, denotes, not corporate raiding in the (generally) legal sense of the Western term, but the illegal grabbing of assets, usually with official connivance. One form of *reiderstvo* was experienced by Hermitage Capital Management: the theft of company assets by policemen.[17] This example involved a Western investor. The case became notorious far beyond

---

14 The military analyst Stephen Blank, however, points out that a re-capitalization of the military has already been delayed and the pressures for it are now very strong. (Response to questions at the ASEES conference panel on Economics and Defense in Contemporary Russia, Washington, DC, 18 November 2011.)

15 A score in 2008 of -0.968 in a range between +2.5 and -2.5, http://info.worldbank.org/governance/wgi/pdf/wgidataset.xls.

16 In the WEF GCR Russia scores well on criteria such as market size and rate of growth and workforce skills.

17 'Testimony of William Browder, CEO, Hermitage Capital Management', US Commission on Security and Cooperation in Europe, 23 June 2009.

Russia because of the death in custody of the lawyer Sergei Magnitskii, who first uncovered the scam. Russian businesses are commoner and less widely publicized targets.

The dubious acquisition of assets is usually conducted with help from pliable courts. This was one ingredient in the Hermitage case. It has also been a feature of actions against the Russian assets of the Norwegian telecoms company Telenor,[18] and against BP in its role as co-owner of TNK-BP.

The role of the state in these phenomena is not simply one of predation. There is also the entrenched view that all wealth and all power stem from the state, so that informal state control is widely seen as in some sense necessary.[19] This seems to be the background to the much-quoted remark of the aluminium tycoon Oleg Deripaska in July 2007: 'If the state says we must give up our companies, we will give them up. I do not separate myself from the state.'[20]

A leading businessman has given the following guidelines for survival: 'Pay your taxes on the due date, neither before nor after. Avoid anything that might be construed as politics, such as public statements. Stay off the inner circle's commercial territory. Keep the inner circle well-informed of your activities.'[21]

Even if one follows this guidance, the Russian business environment is still full of pitfalls. This has inhibited the country's development.

Present and future consequences of a difficult business environment

The main consequences of this difficult environment in Russia are that the small-business sector is comparatively under-developed; competition is weak; incentives to invest in the country are constrained by a lack of confidence in the ability to secure the returns; large private firms are closely held, typically through offshore holding companies; and part of domestic savings is channelled abroad.

Small business

According to official Russian data for 2009, 4.5 million people worked in firms of 1–15 employees, 5.7 million in firms with 15–100 employees, and there were an estimated four million unincorporated sole traders.[22] These are not negligible numbers. It is hardly the case that Russia lacks small businesses. Still, these numbers add up to only about 21% of employment. In Central and West European countries the comparable share is more of the order of 40–50%. Russia is under-endowed with this particular source of economic vigour.

Competition

Several analysts of the Russian economy have noted the extensive impediments to internal competition. One summary measure of the degree of competition is the OECD's product market regulation (PMR) indicator. This combines 18 indicators under three headings: state control, barriers to trade and investment, and barriers to entrepreneurship. The higher the indicator, the more regulation and the less competition there is. The latest data available show that the OECD average for 2008 was 1.340 and the Russian PMR was 3.094. For further comparison, Greece had a PMR of 2.374.[23]

There are some dynamic and competitive Russian companies, despite everything. Examples include Yandex (search engines), Kaspersky Lab (anti-virus software), the X5 retail Group, and Wimm-Bill-Dann (soft drinks and dairy products; recently taken over by Pepsico). But

---

18   Telenor's Executive Vice-President, Jan Edvard Thygesen, posted on the company website a statement including the observation that this was 'yet another escalation of the attempts to steal our VimpelCom shares with the aid of Russian courts' (accessed 20 March 2009; removed from the website after Telenor held on to its assets and reached a truce with its Russian partner; see also T. Dzyadko and A. Golitsyna, 'V Nyu-York za pravdoi' [To New York in search of the truth], *Vedomosti*, 11 June 2009).

19   Exactly how this control works is not clear. Clifford Gaddy and Barry Ickes argue that the key is the monopoly of a (continuing) compilation of the real financial data of Russian business groups, held by Putin and a small circle of his associates, that can be deployed against any tycoon who steps out of line (Gaddy and Ickes, 'Putin's Protection Racket', working paper presented at November 2011 meeting of ASEES in Washington). Why, if this is really the heart of the matter, such flimsy, trumped-up charges were used against Mikhail Khodorkovsky (in both the cases brought against him) is mysterious.

20   *RFE/RL Newsline*, 2 October 2007.

21   Private conversation with author.

22   OECD, *OECD Reviews of Innovation Policy: Russian Federation*, 2011, p. 81.

23   OECD, www.oecd.org/dataoecd/33/12/42136008.xls.

the scope for such companies to thrive is limited. The tendency is for dynamic companies like these to appear in industries that either did not exist at all in Soviet times or were woefully under-developed before 1992. It also helps if the post-Soviet state is no more than minimally involved. Unfortunately, there is a large part of the economy where these conditions do not apply.

Incentives to invest at home

It is a striking feature of Russian economic activity that there has been a net outflow of private capital in every year since the disintegration of the USSR except 2006 and 2007. Figure 2 shows the balance-of-payments current account, where a persistent surplus makes possible an outflow of capital, and the recorded net flows of private capital from 1998 to 2011.[24] In the recovery since 2009 the net outflow has continued. In 2011 it was $84.2 billion.[25]

Between them, Russian firms, households and the state tend to save more than they invest at home. Russia, Poland and Turkey all have similar, moderate ratios of investment (in the broad sense of fixed investment plus the change in inventories) to GDP. In 2010 these percentages were 20.3, 20.8 and 20.1, respectively. The ratios of saving to GDP were, in the same order, 25.1, 16.3 and 13.6.[26] Russia, an emerging economy with considerable potential for investment at home, channels a substantial part of its savings abroad. Poland and Turkey attract more investment than their savings will finance.

This tendency shows up in figures of inward and outward foreign direct investment (IFDI and OFDI) – see Figure 3. Russia is unusual among large emerging economies in that its stock of OFDI has been close in size to its stock of IFDI. China, India, Brazil and South Africa, though all in recent years spawning multinational businesses, exhibit what might, albeit somewhat tendentiously, be termed the more normal pattern of IFDI exceeding OFDI.

The evidence cited here is circumstantial but powerful: the problematic Russian environment creates an incentive for business to 'escape the system': to invest at home on a comparatively modest scale and to place assets and develop businesses offshore on a large scale.

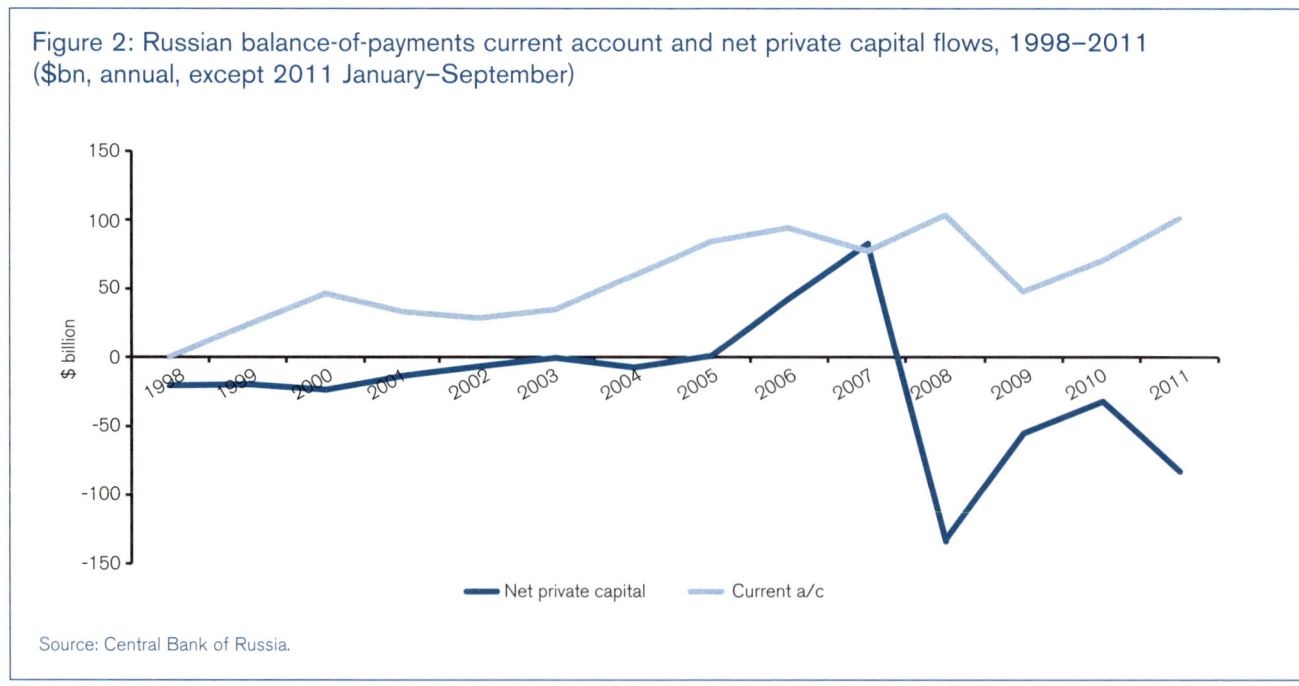

Figure 2: Russian balance-of-payments current account and net private capital flows, 1998–2011 ($bn, annual, except 2011 January–September)

Source: Central Bank of Russia.

24   The current account surplus allows but does not rigidly entail an outflow of capital in this sense. It could in principle be offset entirely by an accumulation of foreign exchange reserves (which would be a minus entry in the balance of payments). In fact, both have occurred.

25   Interfax, citing the Central Bank of Russia, 12 January 2012.

26   IMF World Economic Outlook database of September 2011.

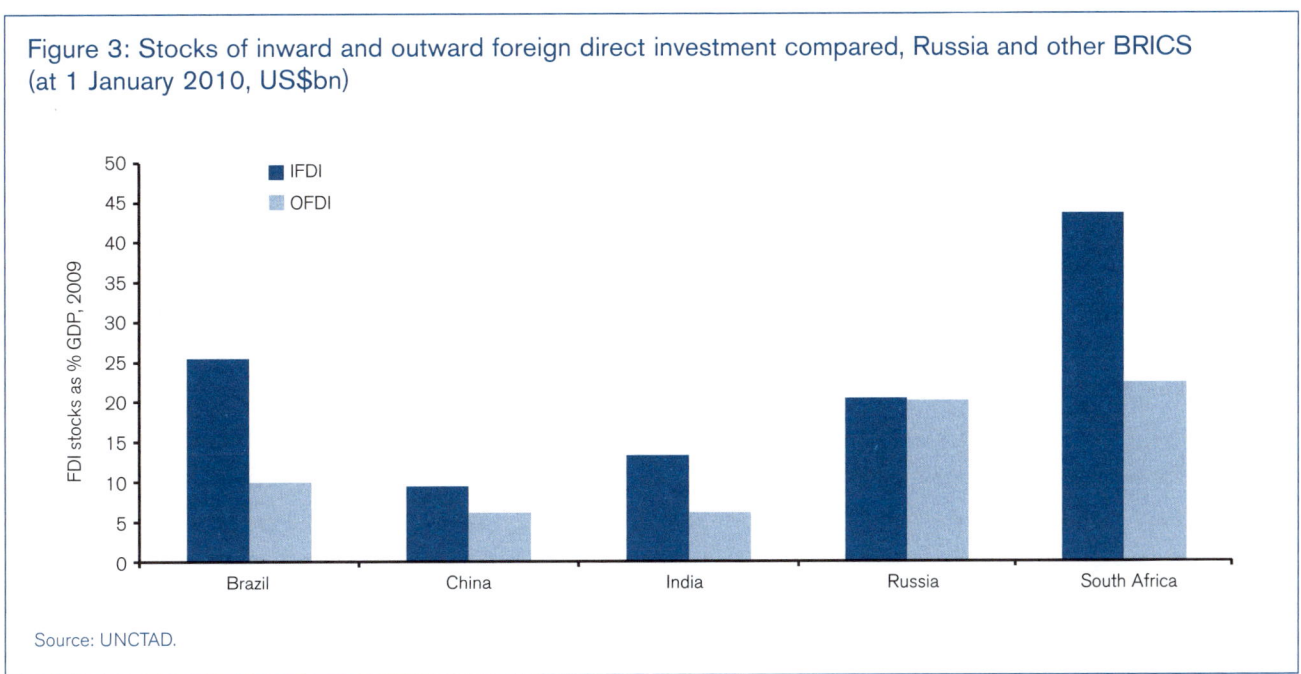

Figure 3: Stocks of inward and outward foreign direct investment compared, Russia and other BRICS (at 1 January 2010, US$bn)

Source: UNCTAD.

Large companies closely held through offshore holding companies

Businesses all around the world use tax havens, but Russian business appears to do so more than most.[27] Many, and very likely most, large Russian firms are closely held (hence the low ratio of turnover to capitalization on Russian stock markets) through offshore holding companies. Vladislav Surkov, until recently an influential presidential aide and now a deputy prime minister, once described Russian tycoons as 'offshore aristocrats'. Table 2 provides some examples of these, their assets and holding companies.

For a long time, the authorities did not seek to change these arrangements. Then in December 2011 Putin launched a campaign against the syphoning-off of funds from state companies (only) to offshore associates. This looks like an attempt at combating the public perception that civil society figures such as Aleksei Naval'niy have a

Table 2: Some offshore aristocrats

Tycoon	Asset	Holding company/ies
Roman Abramovich and Aleksandr Abramov	Evraz Group	Lanebrook, Cyprus
Oleg Deripaska	Rusal	A. Finance, B. Finance, British Virgin Islands
Vladimir Lisin	NLMK	Fletcher Group Holdings Ltd, Cyprus
Aleksei Mordashov	Severstal	Frontdeal Ltd, Cyprus
Viktor Rashnikov	MMK	Mintha Holding Ltd and Fulnek Enterprises Ltd, Cyprus
Suleiman Kerimov	Uralkalii	Kaliha Finance, Cyprus
Viktor Velksel'berg	Renova	Renova Holdings, Bahamas
Mikhail Fridman, German Khan, Petr Aven	Alfa Group	CTF Holdings Ltd., Gibraltar

Sources: *Vedomosti*; company websites; http://ru.wikipedia.org L0ngl3y.

---

27   For more evidence on this see Hanson, 'Russia's Inward and Outward Foreign Direct Investment: Insights into the Economy', *Eurasian Geography and Economics*, vol. 51, no. 5 (2010), pp. 632–53.

monopoly of anti-corruption activity.[28] However, Rosnano, Rosneft and Rostekhnologii appear not to be included among the targets of this campaign, which is being run by First Deputy Prime Minister Viktor Zubkov and Deputy Prime Minister Igor Sechin and two leading statists, and is probably, as Yevgeniya Pis'mennaya has argued, a sham. In any case, the campaign does nothing to address the outflow of capital arranged by private-sector 'offshore aristocrats'.

What is to be done?

A re-acceleration of Russian growth would require a faster rate of increase of fixed investment and more rapid introduction and diffusion of new technology. Russia's present economic institutions do not encourage either of these developments. On the contrary, they curb competition, which forces firms to keep up with new technology, and they curb investment at home in favour of investment offshore.

There has been technological progress but the problem is that there has not been enough of it. The capital stock has been growing at about 3% a year[29] – less than would be desirable, but still an increase – and almost all the new equipment installed has been imported. Insofar as imported equipment embodies more advanced labour productivity levels than existing Russian plant, and insofar as Russian companies use that equipment efficiently, this is a powerful source of productivity growth. However, this particular source of growth is already built into existing patterns of economic activity. It provides fuel for acceleration only if the rate of growth of investment is stepped up.

The faster growth of investment and technological change that is needed cannot be secured by state-led, top-down policies. State-led modernization may have been successful in some countries (such as Singapore or South Korea perhaps) but in Russia the state is a large part of the problem. The question is how to arrive at independent courts, a proper rule of law, sound protection of property rights, and a competitive environment in which small, medium and large firms will operate on a level playing-field, which is so remote from Russian experience.

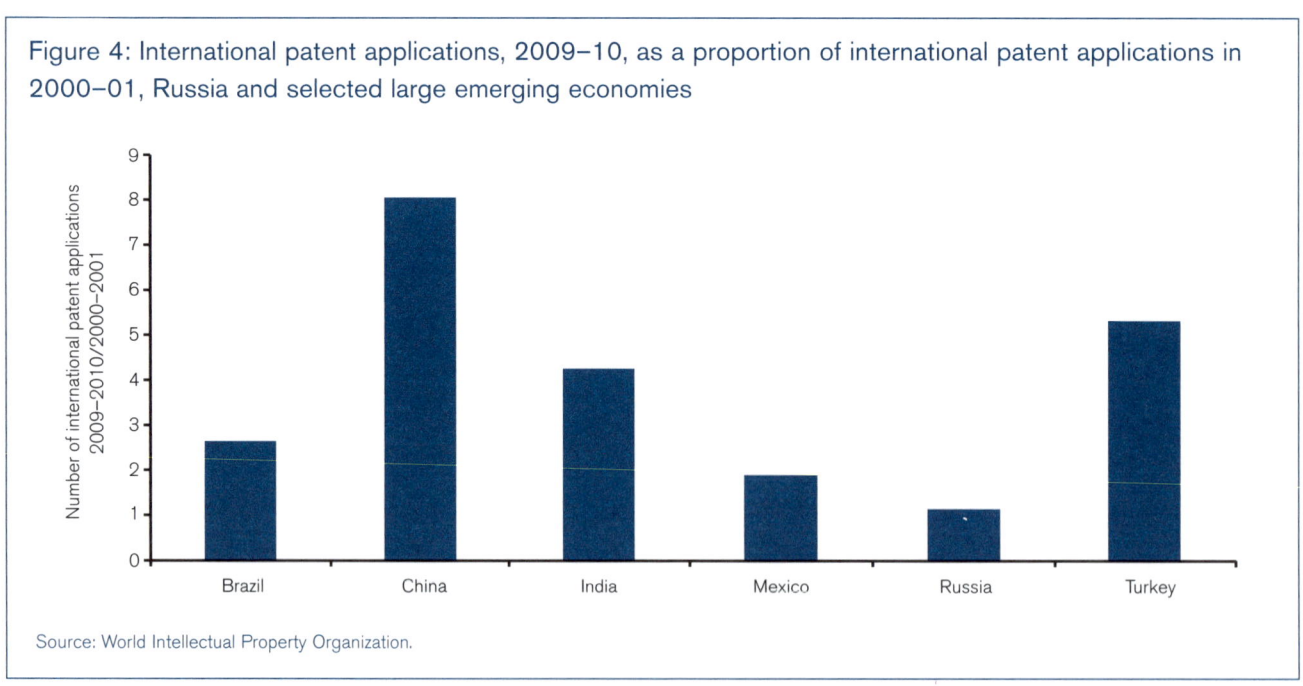

Figure 4: International patent applications, 2009–10, as a proportion of international patent applications in 2000–01, Russia and selected large emerging economies

Source: World Intellectual Property Organization.

28   Maksim Tovkailo, Oksana Gavshina, 'Goskompaniyam i gosbankam pridyetsya rasskazat' o sebe vsye' [State companies and banks will have to declare everything], *Vedomosti*, 11 January 2012; Yevgeniya Pis'mennaya, 'Boyevaya operatsiya Putina po bor'be s korruptsiyei – profanatsiya i pokazukha' [Putin's fight against corruption – profanity and window-dressing], in ibid.
29   Kubinowa, 'Russian Growth Path'.

Economic liberalization would, in time, force companies to acquire and apply new technologies in order to survive and gain market share. At present, the demand for research and development (R&D) is weak. Most research is still financed and carried out by the state. That is to be expected in the case of fundamental scientific research but not for R&D closer to practical application.

Moreover, Russian fundamental science is itself in trouble. In an open letter to the president and prime minister in 2009, a large number of expatriate Russian scientists described it as being in a 'catastrophic' condition.[30] A middle generation of Russian-trained scientists, aged roughly between their early thirties and early sixties, has left for work either in other countries or in other fields in Russia. Research funding is not, for the most part, allocated by peer review of project applications. International involvement is minimal and Russian science is cut off from the wider world of international collaboration. The strength of Russian expatriate science was illustrated by the award of the Nobel Prize for physics in 2010 to Andre Geim and Konstantin Novoselov, for work undertaken at Manchester University. Both reportedly turned down financially attractive offers to spend time working in Russia.

Russian applied science and technology appear to be similarly subdued. Unlike other large emerging economies, Russia's output of international patent applications, for example, has been flat (See Figure 4.) In other words, liberalization needs to extend to science and technology.

Efforts under way

The state modernization campaign is best known for the planned 'Russian silicon valley' at Skolkovo and Rosnano, the company headed by Anatolii Chubais. The only good news here is the involvement of Chubais, an exceptionally gifted economic administrator. The man who, in the aftermath of the Yukos affair and in the middle of Putin's turn to statism, managed to push through the unbundling and partial privatization of electricity supply in Russia should not be underestimated.

Chubais has used Rosnano money to develop, among other things, a venture capital fund that can finance start-ups and to invest in two US bioscience companies on condition they set up divisions in Russia. The eventual presence of several leading international high-tech firms at Skolkovo is encouraging, as far as it goes. But only a more general liberalization, with secure property rights and a state that sets the framework but otherwise keeps out of firm-level decisions, seems capable of reinvigorating the Russian economy.

That is exactly what is recommended in the Interim Report of the experts revising the national 'strategy to 2020'.[31] This states that the old growth model, relying on rising domestic demand propelled by rising oil revenues, has had its day.[32] Growth at or above 5% a year is needed. The key institutional problems that need to be addressed, the report says, are:

- The inequality of rights among market participants;
- Barriers to market entry for new companies;
- The distorting effects of the 'state and monopoly' sectors;
- Excessive and ineffective regulation;
- Corruption; and
- Insufficient restructuring of established firms, which receive state support in one form or another.[33]

The report runs to 517 pages. The reader who makes it to the end will not find an answer to the question, 'How, politically, is this to come about?' The second elephant in the room, alongside the report itself, is the symbiotic relationship between the political elite and the 'inequality of rights', the 'barriers', the 'distorting effects' and the other problems deplored by the report's authors.

---

30   See http://www.hep.soton.ac.uk/~belyaev/open_letter. On the limited success so far of attempts to develop research at Russian universities see Irina Dezhina, 'Developing Research in Russian Universities', at http://www.ifri.org/downloads/ifridezhinarusresearchinuniversitiesjan2011.pdf. On weaknesses in contemporary education generally, see Vladislav Inozemtsev, 'Khoroshee obrazovanie v Rossii – mif' [Good education in Russia is a myth], *Vedomosti*, 3 October 2011.

31   *Promezhutochniy* … 2011 (see note 10 above).

32   Ibid. p. 11.

33   Ibid, p. 26.

Yevgenii Yasin, the doyen of Russian liberal economists, has bravely tried to address the political economy of systemic reform.[34] He argues that step-by-step liberalization is possible. It could begin with some changes in the policy-making team and a declaration of liberal objectives, and proceed through a gradual reduction of federal executive powers, the election of mayors, and independent courts demonstrating an ability to rein in the *siloviki*.[35]

The question remains: why would those in power release their hold on it? Yasin says that one requirement is a grouping of politicians in power who are seriously pursuing a liberal agenda. This is conceivable, but so is resistance to the idea, which could lead to conflict.

Implications for the outside world

If the reinvigoration of the Russian economy requires a strong dose of economic liberalism, and if economic liberalization requires political liberalization, it would be good news for the wider world. Such a scenario, however, is too good to be likely. If a serious push for economic improvement provokes resistance, with the accompaniment of increased political uncertainty and some degree of turbulence, it would not be quite so welcome.

For foreign firms trading with Russia, or investing there, or working with Russian firms outside Russia, a more vigorous economy must in the long run be attractive. In recent years foreign direct investment into Russia has been driven more by the pull of the large and growing Russian market than by access to natural resources. That gravitational pull would be enhanced. If a more vigorous economy was also one with fewer distortions, lower barriers to competition and a firmer rule of law, the attraction would be all the stronger.

Some gradual liberalization under Putin is not impossible. In 2000–03 he presided over a number of substantial measures of market liberalization. Russia's long-delayed accession to the World Trade Organization should now happen in 2012. This will help at the margin because it will extend to the new member at least the rules of a level international playing-field, and it should promote competition within Russia. Even so, radical reform under Putin, even under the pressure of slow growth and with the minor assistance of WTO membership, must be considered unlikely. In the long run the Putinist system is the main barrier to fundamental reform. The policies of countries engaging with Russia should avoid giving help and succour to that system.[36]

Box 1: Could the United Kingdom do more to assist reform?

In the context of the arguments made in this chapter, there are some specific questions that arise for the United Kingdom. It may be that some of its current arrangements and practices provide undue support for the dubious practices of Russian business.

Many tax havens are British crown dependencies. Admittedly, Cyprus, which is not, is the Russian favourite, but many Russian companies use the British Virgin Islands, the Bahamas, Gibraltar and the rest.

Russian companies, not all of them with impeccable reputations, have launched initial public share offerings and been registered on the London Stock Exchange (LSE). Premium LSE listings, making the companies in question accessible to institutional investors, require a 25% free float of shares. This should be rigorously enforced, at the very least.

English lawyers also earn large sums of money acting in commercial cases where the assets and transactions at issue are not only outside English jurisdiction but are located in a murky world without a rule of law.

A more puritanical UK stance on these matters is unlikely, but at the very least the authorities might consider more seriously the messages they are sending.

---

34   'Yevgenii Yasin: Modernizatsiya bez shokovoi terapii' [Yevgenii Yasin: Modernization without shock therapy], *Vedomosti*, 14 October 2011.
35   Mayoral elections would foreshadow competitive elections at higher levels.
36   Some policies that are not directly to do with Russia could have that effect: sending the oil price up by attacking Iran's nuclear facilities, for example.

5. Russia's Geopolitical Compass: Losing Direction

James Nixey

Introduction

With 14 separate land borders, a 58,000 km perimeter, a controversial twentieth-century history and a long-standing legacy of assuming a right to superpower status, Russia needs its external relations to be exceptionally multi-dimensional, sensitive and deft. Sadly, its foreign policy falls short on all counts. Russia has no genuine friends in the international arena, uses its Soviet and Tsarist history as a rationalization for bullying actions beyond its borders, and has a 3–4% share of the world economy, all of which suggest that its self-proclaimed status as a global power is somewhat far-fetched.

It is widely acknowledged that Russia's foreign policy is more than usually linked to domestic factors.[1] Given the analysis in preceding chapters that there can be no substantial change within Russia until there is meaningful change in the structure and conduct of its governing elite, it follows that its foreign policy ambition to be a respected global actor will not meet with success until this happens. That will be all the more the case if the next Russian administration chooses to meet the increasing challenges it is likely to face by tightening its domestic grip. Such a retreat to the past would be likely to come with a more truculent attitude to the outside world.

This chapter examines the prospects for Russia's relations with the four points on its geopolitical compass: the West, Russia's many 'souths' – the Black Sea region and the Islamic world in particular, Russia's Far East and its Arctic north. The chapter then assesses Russia's foreign policy concepts more broadly before drawing some conclusions about where its foreign policy compass is likely to point in the future.

Russia and the West

No matter how far China rises, how problematic Russia's southern regions become or how much potential can be extracted from its Arctic position, Russia will remain Western-oriented (without being pro-Western). The West, for all its faults, its political expediency and its hypocrisy always has been and always will be the yardstick by which Russia measures itself.

Quite correctly, however, Russia does not regard the West as a monolith – and certainly not as all-powerful. Envious of America, disparaging of the EU, antagonistic towards NATO (except in its Afghanistan operations), Russia's Western policy, such as it is, is almost as confused as Western policy is about Russia – but not quite. Russia sets itself up as the 'significant other' in relation to all major Western countries and organizations, whereas the West, with its wider polity, is genuinely divided in its attitudes to Russia – contrast Germany's business-driven acquiescence and Scandinavia's hard-headed scepticism with America's relative indifference.

Moscow will continue to prefer to deal with capitals rather than headquarters – with Paris and Berlin rather than the EU or NATO. As such, it can 'divide and rule', deal with those it wants to and ignore the others, and circumvent the bureaucracy. In some ways this is surprising as some EU bureaucrats in relevant policy-making and advisory roles can be somewhat timid when it comes to Russia. Many in Brussels still believe, falsely, that the EU is more dependent on Russia than Russia is on the EU. The EU's flagship policy towards Russia has been the

---

1   See Neil Malcolm, Alex Pravda, Roy Allison and Margot Light, *Internal Factors in Russian Foreign Policy* (London: Royal Institute of International Affairs/ Oxford University Press, 1996).

empty 'partnership for modernization' – an agreement in name only to promote a Russian fantasy of technological advancement, for which the EU has no appetite, owing to its own current poor economic health and Russia's continued intransigence. Russia, at least, has a more concentrated approach to what it regards as its problems (for instance, difficult neighbours such as Belarus or even Georgia), whereas the EU often lacks such focus.

There are exceptions to the EU's 'Russia weakness', however. One example was the European Commission's unusually brave action in ordering raids on offices of Gazprom subsidiaries in a series of European capitals in September 2011 as part of an investigation into EU anti-trust law violations. Another was the EU's resistance to the Kremlin's desire for a free trade agreement with Europe that would allow more downstream oil and gas activity in Europe by opaque Russian corporate giants, as they try to protect assets from the predatory Russian state. The same also goes for the EU's refusal to countenance a visa-free regime.

The United Kingdom will remain a thorn in Russia's side as wider ties than the purely political keep them together. For as long as the United Kingdom retains a strong Eurosceptic streak (regardless of the party in power), and in the absence of progress on specific issues of disagreement, intergovernmental relations will remain poor. The breaking-off of full diplomatic relations is just a distant possibility, however; one that only a row on an unprecedented scale could cause. Even the murder of Alexander Litvinenko in London in November 2006 and Moscow's subsequent refusal to extradite the chief suspect resulted merely in the expulsion of two diplomats per side and a frosty phase in relations.

Germany, by contrast, desires a further deepening of its already cosy relations with Russia. Unlike most EU countries, it is not especially concerned about its increasing, though still limited dependence on Russian energy (39% of its gas and 36% of its oil come from there)[2] and certainly not with Russia's lack of progress on democracy and human rights. Russia is only too happy to oblige. But Germany's energy picture is changing: oil can be bought reasonably freely on spot markets, and there is less concern about its country of origin. It is pipeline gas with long-term contracts that gives Moscow leverage. But even here, in 2010 gas made up only 23% of German primary fuel consumption (though this is set to increase as the use of domestic nuclear power winds down to zero). And Russian gas accounts for only 9% of German primary fuel consumption.[3] The crux of the German–Russian relationship is, in fact, that some big German companies are closely tied to Gazprom and have had an undue influence on Germany's Russia policy. 'Schroederization'[4] was not just a single episode.

The main threat to German–Russian relations is not any direct political fall-out but Russia's failure to make good on its modernization plans (not least because modernization comes with a political price and because the governing elite is more interested in self-enrichment than in enriching its country). This will hurt energy relations and vital trade from small and medium-sized enterprises in Russia. Germany, as Constanze Stelzenmüller has pointed out, is perhaps the only European country with political capital for leverage in Russia.[5] It is also, presumably, the foreign country with which Vladimir Putin personally has the most affinity. Germany could and should exploit this to greater European advantage, rather than just for its own benefit, thereby ensuring a continued leading role in Europe. Yet with such an obsequious Russia policy, Germany currently lacks political credibility in Europe.

The West's lack of uniformity and current weaknesses, however, suggest paradoxically that Russia will see it as more attractive than before because it is more easily exploitable. Russia knows that it needs Western technology and investment. The hitherto successful use of energy cut-offs and the hostile takeovers of some Western enterprises in Russia to express dislike of other countries' policies have resulted in short-term wins for Russia while

2   OECD/IEA, *Natural Gas Information and Oil Information 2011*.
3   BP, *Statistical Review Of World Energy, June 2011*, derived from p. 41; and with thanks to Philip Hanson.
4   Germany's former Chancellor, Gerhard Schröder, is perhaps the most prominent of Russia's staunch defenders – some would say apologists – abroad.
5   Constanze Stelzenmüller, 'Germany's Russia Question', *Foreign Affairs*, Vol. 88, No. 2, March/April 2009.

the West (slowly) counters with a combination of diversification and protectionist policies. Moscow's dream of energy leverage was never more than that, as Russia needed the revenue as much as the West needed the supply. In fact, energy has become a weakness as it ties Russia to the fluctuating international fortunes of the sector overall. Certainly Russia's energy card has not helped it secure a major international decision-making role.

As noted in Chapter 2, Russia sees itself as a natural analogue (or at least as second only) to the United States in terms of world powers. The US–Russian Bilateral Presidential Commission plays to this vanity (even though it is, in large part, a simple America-to-Russia donor mechanism). This is not an argument for its discontinuation; only an acknowledgment that it is just an unfortunate leftover from US engagement with Russia in the Cold War.

The relationship between Russia and the United States has been defined lately by the Obama administration's attempt at a 'reset', a term that implicitly acknowledges how bad relations became during the final years of the George W. Bush and Vladimir Putin 'Mark I' regimes. Russia never understood that for the United States the reset was less about the relatively unimportant US–Russian relationship and more about giving Washington greater room for manoeuvre in other areas (Afghanistan and Iran above all). In any case, the reset has improved matters little beyond the level of rhetoric. At most, the United States has picked the 'low-hanging fruit' of arms control agreements and over-flight rights (supporting operations in Afghanistan), starkly exposing major differences between the two countries in terms of worldview, intentions and capabilities. A Russia that constantly compares itself to the United States, finds the comparison wanting and carps about American misdemeanours while lacking in self-awareness about its own failings makes for a difficult partner with whom to reset relations on a number of levels. For the United States, the reset was worth trying, but was based on the fundamentally dubious premise that somehow the relationship's deterioration was due to mutual neglect and mistakes on both sides. The record from, say, 2003 to the beginning of the reset in 2009 proves that this is by and large not correct, as Russia's foreign policy rhetoric (exemplified by the Putin's Munich Security Conference speech of 2007) and action (primarily the Georgia war) became increasingly hostile.

Even missile defence cannot be regarded as the mutually beneficial success story for the reset that it is sometimes claimed to be. The US aim is to deploy elements of an ABM system directed against possible new threats from different states, preferably with a degree of Russian acquiescence, but in any case without giving Moscow a right of veto over its use or the ability to override an order to deploy. Russia's goal in the coming years will be to limit the range and therefore the effectiveness of this NATO-controlled system. Meanwhile Russia, which has often used the ABM defence issue to pick a quarrel, is now planning its own separate aerospace defence system (VKO), designed to repel the kind of advanced missiles that only America could have. The planned Russian increase in military spending to 2020 will not be enough to pay for this, but it will be enough for early-warning radar systems and new, upgraded missile systems.[6] But the fragility of the agreement – and the reset more broadly – is underplayed by a US administration desperate to claim foreign policy successes.

Resetting the reset will therefore require substance; but there is little common ground. The United States could and should repeal the Jackson-Vanik amendment, a law that denies permanent normal trade relations (most-favoured-nation status) to any country that restricts emigration and other human rights. (Russia does, however, get a waiver at present and the amendment is the object of a legal challenge in the US.) Repeal may be difficult in the current American political climate, yet the amendment is no longer relevant to today's Russia. A repeal would at least prolong the reset while the United States figures out how to deal with a more assertive Putin – having unwisely ignored him in recent years in favour of the supposedly more 'liberal' Dmitry Medvedev, who was never running Russia's foreign policy anyway.

---

6   For more detailed information, if a rather one-sided analysis, see Ruslan Pukhov, 'Medvedev's Missile Threats are his "Plan B"', *Moscow Times*, 1 December 2011.

Russia's southern underbelly – the Black Sea region and the Middle East

Russia's fragile southern regions and the countries beyond form its weakest flank in terms of security and understanding of the countries themselves (the Islamic ones in particular).

In the Black Sea region, Russia is a declining power, in spite of its 'acquisition' of (and missile-planting in) Abkhazia in 2008, its successful prevention of NATO expansion there and its ability to confuse Western policy after the August war of 2008. In the days of the Soviet Union, the Kremlin controlled 2,935 km of Black Sea coastline. Now, even with Abkhazia, it has jurisdiction over only 685 km. Georgia's mainstream political actors are united in their suspicion of Russia, with little prospect of a reversal. Ukraine's retreat from Western norms and values under President Viktor Yanukovych does not equate to a new-found love for Mother Russia.[7] And even Abkhazia, in the long term, looks set to drift away as Russia's current total economic stranglehold eventually loosens.[8]

In the absence of willing, cooperative or analogous partners in the West or, as will be seen below, the East, Turkey appears a more suitable ally for Russia, considering its emerging extra-regional ambition and its own schism over its geopolitical orientation between East and West. Bilateral relations have been reinforced by an increased number of hydrocarbon and nuclear energy deals.

In the Middle East and North Africa, Russia's stubbornness over sanctions against its more unpleasant allies, owing to its financially compromised position, has revealed a new impotence. As a handful of the region's regimes began to topple in early 2011, Russia became increasingly isolated. Like the rest of the world, it did not realize at the time that Tunisia's revolution was the first domino in a row and, as its interests there are few, it was relatively relaxed about the upheavals. But the Kremlin's voice became increasingly strained and desperate – albeit still ignored – as

other North African regimes fell. As Egypt followed, there was increasing dismay at the domino effect and strong criticism by Medvedev of the protestors in Tahrir Square in April 2011. This was followed, equally improbably and confusingly, by an endorsement of events in Egypt when Russia saw which way the wind was blowing. Other senior figures such as Igor Sechin blamed the West (and even more dubiously, Google specifically) for the uprisings. As the West became increasingly involved in the war in Libya, Russia protested more loudly still (while abstaining from the UN Security Council vote on authorizing the use of force), but it was ignored again as events there spiralled out of control. And in Syria, Russia's intractable opposition to sanctions as the regime clung to power has been its strongest stance of all – supporting President Bashar al-Assad (for historical, financial and stability reasons) when even the Arab League demanded his resignation.[9] It is curious that Russia supports a regime with a presumably short life expectancy, against the tide of events. But Russia's military-industrial complex would suffer commercially if it were seen to bend to Western pressure – especially after Moscow cancelled its contract to supply S-330 missiles to Iran in 2010 – for it still sells weapons to regimes that even the West balks at.

Meanwhile, the longer-term problem of Iran has not turned out as Russia had hoped, which would have been for Iran to be sensitive to Russia's financial ambition there by not becoming an outright international pariah. Russia views Iran just as the West views Russia – as unpredictable and unhelpful. Russia's 2005 diplomatic move offering to dispose of Iran's weaponizable fissile material inside Russian territory was, to its disappointment, rejected by Iran, though not by the West. And yet, just as the West sticks with Russia, Russia sticks with Iran, objecting to additional sanctions and illogically condemning the International Atomic Energy Agency's November 2011 report on Iran's nuclear programme. Indeed Moscow only agreed to the limited sanctions on Iran because they permitted Russia to continue selling

---

7   See Alexander Bogomolov and Oleksandr Lytvynenko, *A Ghost in the Mirror: Russian Soft Power in Ukraine.* Chatham House Briefing Paper, February 2012.

8   See James Nixey, *The Long Goodbye: Waning Russian Influence in the South Caucasus and Central Asia,* Chatham House Briefing Paper, March 2012.

9   Well before Foreign Minister Sergei Lavrov's desperate shuttle diplomacy with Damascus in February 2012, Russia's Middle East Envoy, Mikhail Margelov, met members of the Syrian opposition in Moscow in June 2011, suggesting that Russia does like to keep its options open ('Russian envoy to Africa to meet Syria opposition in Moscow', 10 June 2011, http://en.rian.ru/world/20110610/164549208.html).

the country nuclear power, and to develop its oil and gas sectors. This contradictory policy will surely continue as long as Russia's threat assessment of Iran remains lower than the West's.

It is not just that Russia is torn between mutually exclusive ambitions for a nuclear-weapon-free Iran on the one hand and nuclear assistance to the country on the other. Russia's distaste for American military involvement in the region is counterbalanced by its knowledge that the backlash against the United States resulting from such involvement would be desirable in itself for Moscow and increase world energy prices to Russia's significant economic advantage. In the longer run, however, the more traditional Russian argument that an eventual American–Iranian rapprochement would neuter Russia's historical advantage in the region still holds. But for the more immediate, more visible future, Russia will continue to profit from the region's strategic tension and from its own lack of squeamishness in dealing with unsavoury regimes. The most cynical view can be summarized thus: a nuclear-armed Iran is better for Russia than an American-friendly one.

The post-Arab Spring Middle East and North Africa is disquieting for Russia on several levels. Whether the events in the region are regarded as the beginnings of democratization or as revolution, neither sits comfortably with Russia, which respects long-term stability in others, no matter how harsh the methods used to achieve it. For Russia's leaders, the lessons of Kosovo and their particular understanding of the Orange Revolution in Ukraine and the Rose Revolution in Georgia remain vivid.

Given the unlikelihood of a fully liberal-democratic Middle East and North Africa region in the foreseeable future, Russia will probably be able again to extract some benefit from the strategic uncertainty on which it thrives. The region's new and old regimes will still want weapons and Russia will supply them, just as it has hitherto to Syria, Iran, Libya and Algeria. Russia should gain if it does not sell arms to them too: as Marcin Kaczmarski points out,

this would give it a bargaining chip with the United States that could be stored and used later.[10] However, if these regimes follow an Islamist orientation, Russia may finally have to take sides.

Arms deals, energy sales and genuine security interests (the latter to ensure that the country's increasingly Muslim south is not pushed further into extremism) are, however, relatively small fry for Russia these days. It now sees its interests, somewhat implausibly, as being an arbiter in the region. Cynics would suggest this is more out of the necessity to appear as a great power than out of humanitarian concern. Either way, its limited efforts over Iran and the Israel–Palestine conflict have not gained significant support either in the region or in the wider international community. Russia, perhaps even more than the United States, is simply not considered an honest broker, and Putin's vicious but presidency-boosting 1999 military campaign in Muslim Chechnya have not helped to change this image. Ultimately, Russia's historical ties in the region have not been nearly strong enough to influence events there. It simply has to wait and see whether events turn out in its favour. Here, as in other regions in flux, Russia will continue to lack a coherent strategy while its own system remains so rigid and jars with its increasing desire to be an influential out-of-area actor.

Russia and the East

Russia's desire to project power eastward reveals the greatest gap between its ambition and its capability. The occasional threat to ignore the West and orient itself towards China especially has been exposed as an empty boast, not least by China itself, which regards Russia essentially as an unreliable excavation quarry – and a less important one than Africa or the Persian Gulf at that. Bilateral trade may have increased tenfold in ten years – from $6.2 billion in 2000 to $60 billion in 2010 – but this is primarily due to energy exports.[11] In any case, Russia

---

10   Marcin Kaczmarski, 'Commentary: Russia's Middle East Policy after the Arab Revolutions', Centre for Eastern Studies, Warsaw, 26 July 2011, http://www.osw.waw.pl/en/publikacje/osw-commentary/2011-07-26/russias-middle-east-policy-after-arab-revolutions.

11   *Tamozhennaya statistika vneshnei torgovli Rossiiskoi Federatsii* [Customs Statistics of External Trade of the Russian Federation], Federal Customs Service of Russia, 2000–2010.

cannot help but be concerned about China's rise. China's population is expanding rapidly, with some 132 million people currently in its northern provinces and in Inner Mongolia. Siberia, meanwhile, is becoming depopulated, with 14.8 million people today, spread over 60% of Russia's territory, and a 3,500 km border with both China and Mongolia.[12] Russia simply does the maths concerning this geopolitical and demographic situation, regardless of how paranoid this approach may or may not be. Yet it also keeps relatively silent about its underlying fears over the future of its eastern flank. It is not mentioned in Russia's Strategy for National Security until 2020,[13] though there is a school of thought that says that where NATO is mentioned, China can be read instead. This is reinforced by the fact that most Russian forces are deployed in the east of the country.

Russia will continue to be relatively cooperative with the international community over North Korea, albeit in exchange for concessions elsewhere (and besides, it does not believe the international community will have any effect anyway). As with Iran, Russia probably does not share the West's gloomy threat assessment of North Korea, now under the leadership of Kim Jong Un; but that country is far less important than Iran to Russia, economically, historically and in terms of protecting its reputation. Russia does worry about a revolution forcing North Korean emigrants into Siberia, however.

A proposed trans-Korean gas pipeline project will significantly alter the Asian energy picture, enabling Russia to export gas to South Korea through the North, as will increased shipments of liquefied natural gas should the former project not be realized.

Russia's machinations in the Asian energy sphere, though theoretically complementing Asia's energy requirements, are marred by distrust and motivated by callous opportunism (as shown by the acceleration on the Eastern Gas Programme immediately after the Fukushima disaster of March 2011 in Japan).[14] But it continues to waver over the division of natural gas exports between China and Japan. Bobo Lo argues that Russia is ultimately more interested in having its values accepted by the West than in reorienting towards the East. His concept of an 'axis of convenience' suggests that Russia, with a poor hand, will continue to instrumentalize China in order to gain acceptance and leverage with the West.[15] Russia is not interested in China in and of itself, only as a market and a geopolitical counterweight to the West.

Russia's policy over the Kurile Islands, which are claimed by Japan, can be summed up as 'possession is nine-tenths of the law'. The disagreement between the two countries was ramped up during Medvedev's tenure with a presidential visit and fresh military installations on the islands. This could be interpreted as a signal to others that Russia intends to have a robust presence in East Asia. Japan manages to maintain a twin-track policy in response – full economic engagement with Russia alongside strong criticism of its position. How long this can last before the Japanese realize that Russia is, quite literally, not going to give ground on this issue is hard to say, but history suggests the situation may continue indefinitely.

Russia's aspirations to be an Asian power are ultimately unconvincing. It is putting significant resources into holding the Asia-Pacific Economic Cooperation summit in Vladivostok in December 2013, just as it has done for vacuous Asian multilateral groupings such as the Collective Security Treaty Organization and the Shanghai Cooperation Organization. But Russia's attention will surely wander afterwards (to the Sochi Winter Olympics, the football World Cup and bidding to chair the G20), as *grandes occasions* and spectacle are better suited to the still Soviet mindset than actually achieving something in the Far East.

---

12   *Rossiskiie Statisticheskiie Ezhegodnik* [Russian Statistical Yearbook], multiple years; and Zhongguo tongji nianjian [National Bureau of Chinese Statistics], multiple years.

13   *Strategiya natsionalnoy bezopasnosti Rossiizkoy Federatsii do 2020 goda* [National Security Strategy of the Russian Federation to 2020], http://www.scrf.gov.ru.

14   Shoichi Itoh, *Russia Looks East: Energy Markets and Geopolitics in North-East Asia* (Washington, DC: Centre for Strategic and International Studies, July 2011).

15   Bobo Lo, *Axis of Convenience: Moscow, Beijing and the New Geopolitics* (Royal Institute of International Affairs/Brookings Institution Press, 2008).

Russia and the Arctic North

With 58% of the total Arctic coastline, the bulk of the polar region's admittedly disputed (in terms of size and ownership) energy wealth, and superior navigation routes and infrastructure (primarily icebreakers), it seems hard to imagine that Russia can go wrong in the Arctic, as new technologies emerge and faster trade routes become increasingly accessible. And indeed, with these advantages, Russia has, by and large, played its Arctic hand sensibly thus far. Television-friendly flag-planting, territory-claiming stunts aside, it has gauged that its interests are best served by making use of international law. A near twenty-year disagreement with Norway over the delimitation of the Barents Sea was settled in 2010. Beyond its rhetoric, which alternates between the language of international cooperation and jingoism, Russia's application to the UN Commission on the Limits of the Continental Shelf, claiming exclusivity on a 200-mile outward extension of the Lomonosov and Mendeleev nautical shelves (with about 1.2 million sq km of seabed), backed up by its own geological evidence, has been pending for over a decade. The delay is due, in large part, to the massive implications of the claim: if successful, it would give Russia a 45% share of the Arctic.

However, Russia's policy has hard edges too, particularly in the military sphere with deployments of new Arctic brigades. Air and sea military exercises have been designed to test Norway's patience and contrast uncomfortably with Russia's pleas for international Arctic cooperation and a rules-based approach. A Russian coal-mining settlement on the Norwegian Arctic island of Svalbard is clearly uneconomical, probably being maintained for intelligence-gathering and as a 'reminder' of Russia's presence beyond its internationally recognized territory. Norway maintains a calm outward appearance, but it worries that the region's only non-democracy could be a serious spoiler of cooperative management of regional issues in the region.

Russia acknowledges the need for Western assistance to extract the Arctic's mineral wealth from under the ice and water but it has been indecisive at best and duplicitous at worst over its choices of foreign partners for exploration and extraction. For the development of the Shtokman field in the Barents Sea and the exploration of the South Kara Sea, the Western partners with the appropriate technological experience have not always been the most politically expedient for Russia. This has resulted in frustrating vacillations for bidders uncertain of the terms and conditions to be met in order to win and maintain contracts with the Russian energy giants.

The Arctic is becoming globalized. In addition to the eight countries with territory inside the Arctic Circle, China, Japan, South Korea and the EU are emerging players there too. In contrast to its attitude towards the other post-Soviet regions to Russia's south and west, Russia has thus far made little attempt to prevent this globalization. This may be because the Arctic states are harder to bully. But it is also due to a calculation that Russia's natural advantages (primarily its sheer size), combined with a few robust reminders that the Arctic is a 'priority' region, should allow it, in time, to extract tangible benefit from its geographical and geological good fortune in an area estimated to contain some 75% of the world's undiscovered oil and gas reserves, as well as metals, fish and shipping lanes.

Beyond the compass: concepts, pride and prospects for foreign policy

If it is a truism that internal factors drive Russian foreign policy strategy, then it is also commonly accepted – including by Russia itself – that its vast mineral wealth is one of the key instruments of that strategy. Unreliable and threatening though it can be, Russia is nonetheless the world's top oil producer and holds nearly one-quarter of the world's proven natural gas reserves.[16] And for all the concerns other countries have about Russia, it still is looked on favourably by comparison with the world's other resource-rich areas or countries such as the Middle East, West Africa and even Venezuela.

---

16   *BP Statistical Review of World Energy*, 2011.

The Kremlin's ambitions for the other former Soviet states once firmly within its grasp have been well documented recently.[17] For post-imperial Russia, dealing with these independent countries does not really constitute foreign policy – it is seen as an extension of its domestic vision. Ukraine, for example, is not even a nation, according to Vladimir Putin (as captured in a conversation with George W. Bush in 2008).[18] Putin's rehashed vision of a 'Eurasian Union', signed so far with just Belarus and Kazakhstan, and due to come into full effect in 2015, is ultimately just another post-Soviet attempt at a Soviet-style integration project. It will surely be stymied by Kazakhstan's desire to break free from being viewed as a purely Central Asian power and by Belarus's unreliability – and particularly when the leaders of those two countries depart from the scene. Nonetheless, having announced it so dramatically, Putin can be expected to push this union in a second presidency. The more compromised post-Soviet states – perhaps Kyrgyzstan, Tajikistan and Armenia – may even capitulate and join, but overall enthusiasm is low, except of course in Russia.

If Russia did regard its policies towards other former Soviet states as foreign policy, it could claim a few more concrete successes. These would include the extension of the lease of the Black Sea fleet base in Sevastopol (now more vulnerable owing to a disgruntled Ukraine increasing the ground rent) and that of the Gyumri base in Armenia, and the probable blocking of the Nabucco pipeline across the Caucasus (which would bypass Russia). Russia could even lay claim to having contributed considerably, through a rare display of diplomatic skill, to avoiding a war between Armenia and Azerbaijan in Nagorno-Karabakh, at least so far. Russia will probably continue to achieve similar successes – often viewed dubiously, occasionally favourably, by the West – ensuring that it will remain a significant player in the post-Soviet space, while failing to prevent the area's overall globalization. Russia wins battles but it is losing the war.

Propping up friendly – i.e. autocratic – regimes in its immediate vicinity (and beyond in the Middle East) makes it easier for Russia to do business with them. It does not expect Western assistance in this, of course; it merely wants other powers not to interfere. The West believes, at least nominally, in the right of all former Soviet countries to decide their own geopolitical orientation. This is in direct contradiction to Russian policy. For all its signatures of relevant agreements in the 1990s, such as the Charter of Paris, Moscow has simply not accepted the concept of a 'Common Neighbourhood', let alone the post-Soviet countries' freedom of geopolitical orientation.

The question for the West is not what it says in response to Russian actions, but what it does. As long as the West largely upholds its values (even if some political expediency or 'pragmatism' is inevitable), Russia's attempts to maintain its sphere of influence are doomed to fail as the other former Soviet states will not be able to resist looking to the West, in spite of its current weakness and Asia's economic rise. Western soft power remains strong, even if its economic power is now open to question. Also bound for failure, eventually, are Russia's attempts to hinder the democratization of the states within that nominal sphere. This will remain a key source of tension for as long as the current internal system is in place in Russia.

The question is how far the West is willing to go to defend these principles in its geopolitical game of 'chicken' with Russia. Merely complaining about Russian interference in other post-Soviet states is relatively safe for the West, allowing it, at least, to stay on the moral high ground. The same is pretty much true for its backing of the creation of alternative energy routes to those crossing Russian territory. But the high ground seems to be enveloped in fog when it comes to material support for the post-Soviet states. Defence assistance or helping them to militarize is a moral dilemma when those countries are far from democratic and when there exists the possibility that the West's weapons might later be used to oppress internal revolution or democratic opposition. In the case of Georgia it could

---

17   See Nixey, *The Long Goodbye*; Bogomolov and Litvinenko, *The Ghost in the Mirror*; and Agnia Baraskunaite Grigas, *Russian Influence in the Baltic States: Legacies, Coercion, and Soft Power* (forthcoming 2012), all in the Chatham House series 'The Means and Ends of Russian Influence Abroad'.

18   Reported conversation between Putin and Bush at the NATO summit in Bucharest, April 2008, http://www.kommersant.ru/doc/877224.

be argued that defence assistance is futile anyway as Russia will always have overwhelming military superiority against it. Russia is increasing its defence spending by 60%, from 1.264 trillion roubles ($42 billion) in 2010 to more than two trillion roubles ($66.3 billion) in 2013.[19]

Aside from in its dealings with North Korea and the former Soviet states where it has on occasion played a broadly positive role (e.g. peacekeeping after the Tajik civil war in 1991 and mediating in Nagorno-Karabakh more recently), Russia has yet to prove that it can play a more constructive role across the globe – and that its actions are not always motivated by self-interest but at least sometimes by altruism. Russia's policies on the larger international problems it aspires to be involved in are almost always motivated by self-interest (this is not to imply that the West's actions never are, which is unarguable) and this limits its ability to make a substantial impact on the world stage. The current stand-off at the UN Security Council, with Russia vetoing its resolution calling for President Assad to stand down, is but the latest example. Its desperate attempts at diplomacy with Syria at the beginning of 2012 have, in fact, isolated Russia yet further – and far more than China. Russia, then, can only be considered a regional power, not a global one. It is still capable of gaining attention, but not critical influence.

Conclusion

A new Putin presidency will undoubtedly occasionally contain harsh rhetoric and recriminations against the West, aimed in part at impressing a domestic audience. In August 2010, Putin remarked that his 2007 Munich speech had been useful in asserting Russia's authority on the international stage.[20] Such a statement suggests that he is unlikely to add many softer touches to his foreign policy. The Georgia war happened under Medvedev's nominal reign, but it had Putin's approval at the very least. Yet in spite of the tactical victory and international isolation the war brought Russia, a turn to xenophobia and an extreme

fortress mentality are as unlikely as a shift to liberal democratic values feeding into Russian foreign policy. The picture will inevitably become even more confused as Russia enters clubs like the World Trade Organization and pushes for a free trade agreement with the EU, while also promoting the Customs Union Treaty with as many other ex-Soviet countries as possible. Similarly, it will partake in big multilateral events but threaten to withdraw from treaties such as the new START and continue to point Russian missiles in Kaliningrad at American defence systems. In sum, Russia will carry on its search for a unique voice in international matters, but probably succeed only in looking like the spoilt child at the party.

The West's attractiveness may be declining, but so is Russia's. Russia is a declining power in relative and possibly in absolute terms. Foreign policy decline is an element of the picture of unravelling stability at home. A neo-liberal empire, the 'Russian Idea', the 'historically conditioned sphere of mutually privileged interests', the 'R' in BRIC, pan-Eurasianism, neo-Eurasianism, the Eurasian Union and even the Russian concept of Eurasia itself are all, ultimately, one and the same thing – symptoms of Russia's desperate attempts to hold on to great-power status. And they are all self-deceiving fantasies.

Russia's size, history, economic weakness and over-ambition will continue to undermine its foreign policy. While the world's largest country is unlikely to either prosper or implode, it will come under strain unless its government addresses a series of interlocking problems. But that does not imply that its foreign policy is likely to change in the foreseeable future. It will remain full of bluster, yet unable to command respect. Russia will be seen as a failure at home, as its lack of great-power status becomes increasingly evident, and as a failure abroad, as its neighbours slip from its embrace and the world's stronger and more mature powers continue to pay it lip service, but ultimately ignore it. This report warns throughout that Russia's stability is at risk as another presidential spell for Putin nears. But for the Kremlin, irrelevance abroad is almost as horrifying as the spectre of the regime's mortality.

19   Reported in RIA-Novosti, 30 July 2010, http://en.rian.ru/mlitary_news/20100730/160003543.html.
20   Interview with Vladimir Putin, *Kommersant* daily, 30 August 2010.

6. Conclusion

The return of Vladimir Putin to Russia's presidency is intended by the country's ruling elite to ensure that the system developed over the past twelve years continues without fundamental change. Russia's political structures will look, in formal terms, much the same after the 2011–12 electoral cycle as they did before it began.

There will be little immediate economic pressure on Russia's rulers to change their accustomed courses either. The longer-term economic outlook is, however, troubling. The population has not been prepared for the difficult structural changes that would be needed to address that, and there is nobody within the current or prospective ruling elite with the will or authority to provide the determined, sustained and relatively liberal political leadership essential for such transformation.

This is not to rule out useful adjustments being made, but moving much beyond the cosmetic would directly threaten the interests of Russia's rulers. The Kremlin, moreover, depends for its purposes on a corrupted bureaucracy of limited competence. Without accountability that would have to reach to the top of the hierarchy, the 'vertical of power' created by Putin will continue to deteriorate.

These factors alone would leave Russia vulnerable to shock, whether external or internal. The break that happened in 2011 and the early months of 2012 between a large part of the educated urban population and the small group of leaders who have held onto power since 2000 was a major shift for the worse in a crisis of the governing system. In any country, such a break would be difficult to repair. The prospect of Russians recovering their confidence in Putin's leadership now looks remote.

A re-elected Putin and his associates may be tempted to seek to renew their grip on power through repressive measures. But that strategy is unlikely to succeed for long, even if it is buttressed by appeals to nationalist or ethnic prejudices, and supported for a time by budgetary bribes.

The Russian people are growing away from the narrowly based regime that has determined their lives in recent years. What they and the outside world face is an increasing challenge to a regime apparently incapable of delivering the radical change required to cope with the pressures that threaten its structures.

It will matter greatly to the West, and particularly to Russia's fellow Europeans, that the further erosion and eventual replacement of Russia's existing regime should be peaceful, not violent. There are those within Russian society, and some within the broader governing structures, who may eventually come to wish for a peaceful transformation in their own interests, and to find a way to work for it.

Russia's 2011–12 electoral cycle has therefore been the latest stage in a continuing process of deterioration, not the start of a renewal, as some in the West might hope. It is this perception that informs the guiding principles suggested throughout this report (and set out in the Executive Summary) for how the West should respond to a new Putin presidency.

www.chathamhouse.org